The Origins
of
Sheffield Wednesday

Jason Dickinson

AMBERLEY

First published 2015

Amberley Publishing
The Hill, Stroud
Gloucestershire, GL5 4EP

www.amberley-books.com

British Library Cataloguing in Publication Data.
A catalogue record for this book is available from the British Library.

ISBN 978 1 4456 1952 1
E-book ISBN 978 1 4456 1970 5

Typesetting and Origination by Amberley Publishing.
Printed in the UK.

Contents

Acknowledgements

I would like to express my thanks to Tom Poad, Jenny Stephens and all at Amberley Publishing for their help in getting this 'labour of love' to the bookshelves, and also to Sheffield Wednesday Football Club, especially communications director Trev Braithwait.

Also thanks to those friends and acquaintances who supplied images and additional information, including Clive Nicholson, Paul Whitaker, Lee Hicklin, John Brodie, Peter Law, Neville Wright (The Wednesday Cricket Club), Andrew Williams (Marsden Cup) and also to my wife, Michelle, for her patience as I spent countless hours in my little office trying to piece together the manuscript.

As with all my works on Sheffield Wednesday, thanks must again go to the staff at Sheffield Central Library and Sheffield Archives, where I have spent almost two decades of my life researching the club's history.

However, the biggest thanks must to go to census and birth records expert Alan Alcott. Without his diligent and ceaseless research I would simply have been unable to produce this book to the level of detail that has finally been achieved.

The Wednesday Anthem

Men of glory famed by story
Now recall your football glory
As your fathers did before ye
Play up Wednesday Boys

Thee from hill and valley
See supporters rally
Friends are here from far and near
To see the Wednesday rally

Play the game and all that's in it
To the last deciding minute
For the cup and may we win it
Play up Wednesday Boys

Introduction

It would be remiss, when covering the pre-Football League era of Sheffield Wednesday Football Club, not to chronicle the formation and impact made by the original Cricket Club back in early nineteenth-century Sheffield and the social conditions which caused both cricket and football to become popular pastimes during the Victorian age. The game of cricket was first played in southern England back in the sixteenth century and slowly gained popularity to become the national sport by the end of the eighteenth century, with the world famous Marylebone Cricket Club (MCC) forming in 1787. The forerunner of today's Yorkshire County Cricket Club actually started life in Sheffield before that date, being founded around 1751, but it was not until the Victorian age that the sport became widely played and grew in popularity as a spectator sport – the town of Sheffield being the centre of the pastime in northern England. High stakes gambling fuelled the expansion of the game and, early in the 1800s, Sheffield was no different; with such barbaric pastimes, to modern eyes, as cock fighting, bear bating and dog fighting being replaced by the new sport. It would perhaps surprise many to know that the early days of cricket in Sheffield, and around England, were fuelled by stake money as teams met for whatever 'pot of gold' had been arranged between the relevant parties. It was also somewhat ironic, when you consider the furore surrounding the onset of professionalism in the game of football in the 1880s, that professional cricket players quickly became a common sight on the village greens and fields as the 'moral guardians' of Victorian society helped to pull the common working man away from the aforementioned inhumane sports of yore – the town trustees often paying the professional players to entertain the populace.

The first game reported in the local press was a works match, played for a stake of eleven guineas, in October 1802, while it was also noted that in October 1805 Hallam beat Stannington by an innings and 52 notches – in those days, runs were recorded by cutting notches in a piece of wood (fans could be seen walking to grounds with sticks in their hands) while each over consisted of four balls, a number that only increased to five in 1889. Games were also recorded in the town of Sheffield in 1815 and 1818, both involving Hallam, with the steady growth of club cricket helped by the closure of the town's racetrack, matched in turn by the aforementioned gambling with handicap, sweepstake and challenge matches all becoming widespread. Handicap betting involved both clubs subscribing to a pool with a joint committee assessing the strength of each side and deciding upon the number of players – sometimes eleven would face twelve or more. A sweepstake match often saw half a dozen clubs subscribe between £10 and £25, with a mini knock-out competition held to decide the winner. A challenge game was simply two sides of equal numerical strength battling in a winner takes all encounter. In the early part of the nineteenth century though, 'single wicket' cricket was more popular than the standard format of the game as two individuals faced one another. Both players had the same set of men in the outfield and the winner was simply the man that amassed the greater score in two innings. Generally though, it was the local taverns that benefited most from these games as most of the money ended up in their coffers! Somewhat strangely, by the end of the nineteenth century, attitudes to the game of cricket had moved almost totally in the opposite direction, with even local league cricket frowned upon by many as an evil detriment to the spirit of the game.

As the game grew in the town, William Woolhouse was heavily involved in the opening of Sheffield's first top-class cricket enclosure. In partnership with his father-in-law, George Steer, the Darnall Cricket Ground was opened on 26 August 1822 with a Sheffield versus Nottingham game. Advertisements for the match stated that 'for full accommodation of supporters extensive platforms have been erected around the field'; a 1s charge was the basic entrance fee while 2s and sixpence gained entry into the low green room. The ground, which was 2 miles from the centre of the town, covered around 5 acres of freehold land and a main stand measuring 54 feet x 18 feet, which was later turned into a dwelling house. The site would also contain a public house, called the Manor House, with various outbuildings and gardens completing the venue. Sadly, the collapse of a spectator stand, in the opening game, caused its temporary closure until the New Darnall Cricket Ground, built on the same site, grew from the ashes – late in 1822, Sheffield cricketers played a benefit game for those injured. Incidentally, the aforementioned George Steer came to a mysterious and somewhat suspicious end as his body was dragged from the Sheffield Canal in November 1827. Two witnesses heard a splash soon after George had left a tavern, but the inquest recorded a verdict of 'found drowned' despite his pockets having been seemingly rifled. The year before his untimely demise, Darnall CG hosted one of the greatest matches in the history of

Sheffield cricket, which almost immediately afforded legendary status to Wednesday player Tom Marsden. The game was a Sheffield/Leicester XI versus the County of Nottingham, played over three days in July 1826, for 200 guineas. The fixture attracted an unprecedented 30,000 fans and saw Marsden take 4-54 in Notts' first innings as they were reduced to 101. In reply, the combined side scored a massive, by early nineteenth-century standards, 379 with Wednesday man Jem Dearman scoring 27. However it was the astonishing batting display of Marsden that stole the headlines as he scored an amazing 227. His tally included only two fours (demonstrating his remarkable patience) and he went on to take another two wickets in the Notts second knock as they were bowled out for 75 runs.

The Darnall ground quickly fell into disrepair, hosting its last major fixture in 1828 and being offered for sale in April 1830, after Woolhouse took over the running of the newly built Hyde Park Cricket Ground, which opened in 1826 at a not inconsiderable cost of £4,000. The new enclosure, three quarters of a mile from the town's marketplace, was built high on the hillside, close to the modern day Park Hill flats, and had space for up to ten matches to be played at one time. Sheffield's second major cricket and sporting venue – pony racing, athletics, pigeon shooting and wrestling were also activities enjoyed at the ground – sat in just over 5 acres of land, which was on a twenty-one-year lease from the Duke of Norfolk, commencing on 25 March 1826, at a yearly rent of £16. A lofty stone wall surrounded the playing area while a 'large and commodious' stone gallery extended the whole length of the south side. In addition, there was also a further 812 square yards of land, on the west side of the field, which was also leased from the Duke of Norfolk at £3, 3s per annum. Upon this stood a large stone-built tavern, which offered sixteen viewing windows and a 21-yard gallery on the roof, while also contained within the structure were long rooms, bedrooms, a kitchen and a bar. It was without doubt a major step in the construction of sporting venues, and the new ground witnessed many memorable games over the years with the Sheffield CC versus Nottingham CC in 1830 being the inaugural first-class fixture. The first game played under the banner of Yorkshire County Cricket Club was also held there, in September 1833, when a Norfolk side faced what was generally referred to as Sheffield Cricket Club – every player in that first 'county' team was from Sheffield, with the county title believed to have been adopted to match the county status of the visitors. A total of twenty first-class games were played on the ground until June 1853, including the first ever Yorkshire versus Lancashire game in July 1849, but the facilities slowly degenerated after the sad passing of Woolhouse – the venue was offered for auction in June 1836.

Wednesday Cricket Club

WEDNESDAY CRICKET CLUB OFFICIALS 1820–92

President (known)	Tenure
William Stratford	1820-
George Dawson	1827
George Hardesty	1828
George Dawson	1829
John Southern	1830
Edward Jackson	1838
H Bolsover	1841
E Earnshaw	1843
H Hunt	1846
Richard Gillott	1848
William Stratford	1851-56
Richard Gillott	1857-63
Benjamin Chatterton	1863-67
Frank S Chambers	1867-70
Henry Hawksley	1870-87
Henry Stratford	1887-89
William Tasker	1889-

Secretary (known)	
E Charles	1837
William Hill	1838
H Fish	1839
A Earnshaw	1841
Francis Hawke	1846-51
Joseph Lockwood	1852-54

H Bannister	1854-55
Thomas Frith	1855-56
John Tasker	1856-59
George Skinner	1859-63
Thomas Anderson	1863-69
John Marsh	1869-72
Tom Cawthron	1872-74
Thomas Anderson	1874-75
Sydney Stratford	1875-77
William Littlehales	1877-80
William Fretwell	1880-84
Harry Pearson	1884-89
J. H. Stainton	1889-91
Percy Bowker	1891-

Although no contemporary records exist to prove the actual formation date of Wednesday Cricket Club, it is commonly believed that in 1820 six local businessmen became the founding fathers of the club. The club's minute books from the mid-nineteenth century do not, unfortunately, mention a definitive year of birth, but various other published evidence does exist with the story of the cricket club, written by long-term member Lance Morley in 1896, categorically stating the year of formation as 1820, confirmed by long-serving member Henry Stratford (son of the club's first president, William), whose personal record of old Sheffield cricket fixtures gave particulars of a Wednesday match played in that year. A formation year of 1816 is mentioned, however, in an article published in *Bells Life* in 1842, but no evidence has been found to either prove or disprove this date so it would be sensible to conclude that 1820 was indeed the year when Wednesday was born. This date is further substantiated by the Annual General Meeting of 1876, where it was stated that the club was in its fifty-sixth year. The six sporting enthusiasts who formed the original club have, however, been passed into history, with all being described as 'little mesters' – a common description in the nineteenth century for a 'master or owner'. The men in question – George Dawson, George Hardesty, Thomas Lindley, John Southern, William Stratford and William Woolhouse – were all linked by a Wednesday half day, which was a practice in Sheffield that only died away relatively recently, and Wednesday were one of several local sides formed in the town in the early part of the century, along with the Monday, Tuesday, Thursday and Friday Cricket Clubs. Along with Wednesday, only Hallam Cricket Club, formed in 1804, has survived from those days. Unfortunately, very little is known about the early years of Wednesday CC as back in the 1820s the three main Sheffield newspapers

– the *Independent*, *Mercury* and *Iris* – were only published weekly and the game of cricket only appeared in their pages when Sheffield Cricket Club faced another town in an advertised game. The now established Wednesday was seemingly first given column inches in June 1826 when it was reported that the Darnall Wednesday Club beat the Friday Club in a two-inning game played at Darnall, with Wednesday scoring 84 and 65 to their opponents 39 and 99 to win by 11 runs; Dawson and Woolhouse stood as umpires. In May 1827, it was reported that a large number of members gathered at the Darnall Cricket Ground on a Wednesday of course – to officially open the new season and shake off the winter cobwebs. It was reported that around twenty to thirty members of the club took to the field before noon while the afternoon saw the 'match players' at the wicket, including legendary Wednesday batsman Marsden, which in turn led to the 'outside men breathing freely' – a nineteenth-century description for the nominated fielders getting somewhat of a run around chasing the ball! After donning their whites for the first time, around forty members then sat down to dinner with Dawson presiding. He alluded to the 'originality and importance of the club' and that for 'himself and friends' expressed his determination to support the noble game of cricket. The evening continued with a variety of songs and toasts to launch the club's seventh summer in fine style. A few weeks later, MCC suggested a series of 'test matches' be played around the country to resolve the issue of whether overarm bowling should be allowed. The first game took place at the Darnall grounds and with the excitement of 'dangerous' overarm bowling, crowds flocked to see an England side, including Marsden, beat Sussex by seven wickets. The venue also staged a grand fireworks display organised by Mr Mortimer of the Royal Gardens, with the public reassured that no harm would come to them if they attended. It was also notable that Woolhouse was the signatory on an announcement, in June 1827, that the Hyde Park Cricket Ground intended to form two clubs, The Amateurs and The Players, for 'practising the amusement of cricket'. Meanwhile, a Wednesday junior side lost against a Hyde Park team at the new ground before the season ended in mid-October, when around thirty members enjoyed a 'very excellent' dinner provided by Woolhouse. The club president testified the many obligations the lovers of cricket owed to Mr Steer for providing one of the best grounds in the country (Darnall) before songs were sung and toasts made to bring the curtain down on another progressive season. For the time being Wednesday stayed loyal to Darnall CG, and in May 1828 it was noted that 'the married men had no peace after losing to the single men' in the opening practice game, while in late October the members of the 'old and respected club' dined at the Theatre Tavern, Arundel Street – home of member Thomas Wiley. The 1829 season started with an opening game and dinner at Darnall, while generally inter-club practice games were the norm with July seeing a game between players of the first and second half of the alphabet. A few weeks later, an understrength Wednesday side lost at Ripon where the local scribe alleged that the 'Wednesday players were ill-mannered in contempt for their rivals', while in early October the farewell game and closing dinner was held at the Darnall Cricket Ground with famous Wednesday men Woolhouse and Marsden donning their whites in a match that 'embraced all the talent of the town and neighbourhood'.

WILLIAM HENRY WOOLHOUSE

Without doubt, William Woolhouse had the biggest influence of any one individual on the game of cricket in early nineteenth-century Sheffield, being recognised as the first 'father' of the sport in the town. Born in Sheffield on 21 January 1791, he gleaned a love of cricket during his formative years and emerged as an outstanding left-handed batsman and bowler. In total he made seventeen first-class appearances, after making his debut in the Sheffield/Leicester game against Nottingham in 1826, and appeared for an England XI in 1828. He also appeared for Yorkshire CCC in their first ever game, against Norfolk in 1833, scoring 31 runs for his county.

Away from sport, he began his working life in the cutlery trade and was working as a small merchant in 1820 when he was one of the founding members of Wednesday CC – running a table knife manufacturing business on Carver Street. Woolhouse, who was a broad and imposing man over 6 feet tall, married his wife Mary in 1829 whose father, George, was publican of the Cricket House Inn at Manor Hill. His father-in-law and William were instrumental in building and running both the Darnall and Hyde Park Cricket grounds, which provided the Sheffield cricketing fraternity with their first top-class facilities.

In later life he became a publican, but his story had a sad ending as William suffered from a spinal complaint and travelled to London to seek a cure. Unfortunately he was unsuccessful, and after missing his horse coach back home he took lodgings, only to pass away during the night on 14 July 1837, aged just forty-six. Tragically, for such a colossus on the Sheffield sporting scene, he was buried in an unmarked grave in All Hallowes churchyard, London, which gave no indication of the pivotal individual that lay beneath.

Move to Hyde Park and
the Marsden Trophy

The 1830 season saw a move to Hyde Park – William Woolhouse having become the proprietor in January – with a 'spirited match' between the married and singles before all the members socialised long into the evening. A two-day game at Ripon was won comfortably, while, with no football to squeeze the game into specific months, Wednesday continued to play well into October, announcing a two-day game against 'Eleven of the County of York' at Hyde Park. Charges were set at threepence for general admission and sixpence for the saloon area of the ground, although the game proved to be one-sided, with a brilliant display of bowling from Marsden – he took twelve wickets – resulting in the visitors scoring only 92 in their two innings, Wednesday winning by 143 runs. The increasing popularity of cricket was also reflected by a news story that was effectively appealing to parents and guardians to stop their children playing the sport in the street as a few windows had been broken by the wooden balls they were using.

GEORGE HARDESTY

Born in Sheffield around 1777/78, George Hardesty worked as a cutler from his Rockingham Street factory in the heart of the town manufacturing solid silver and silver-plated knives and forks. After being one of the six founding fathers of Wednesday CC, he remained an active member and served as President in the late 1820s. Despite being declared bankrupt in February 1838 and January 1840, he recovered to trade into the 1850s while he also continued to don his whites in the summer months – he was noted playing in an over sixties game in August 1838, where his bowling was of such a high standard that he took all ten wickets of his opponents' second innings! Unlike the vast majority of his contemporaries, he lived a long life and reached the grand old age of eighty-three before passing away at his Sheffield home on 18 June 1860.

The following summer saw Wednesday take the unprecedented step of advertising their opening game of the season, played on Wednesday 11 May 1831. This was because the traditional post-game dinner would see local hero Marsden presented with a silver cup to celebrate his remarkable feats on the cricket pitch. Subscriptions had raised enough money to commission a fine trophy made by Sheffield silversmith Messers Smith and Hoult and weighing 50 ounces, and all members and admirers of cricket in general were invited to purchase tickets at a cost of 2s 6d from Mr Wright (at the Yellow Lion), Marsden, Yorkshire cricketers or from Woolhouse at the Hyde Park Ground. Upon the fine trophy was an inscription:

> Presented to Thomas Marsden, May 11, 1831 by the friends and admirers of cricket, in token of their estimation of his undeviating integrity in all public matters, his first rate talent in every department of the game, of his unwearied diligence and undaunted resolution in the field and as a trophy of the distinguished success which has attended his exertions in that noble and manly exercise.

In June 1831, Wednesday started what was hoped would be regular fortnightly practice games, with principal club members Rollins, Smith, Marsden and Woolhouse all present for the first such day. Games against other clubs were, however, still being organised, with Wednesday losing by a solitary run to the Thursday Club.

WILLIAM STRATFORD

The family name of Stratford is inexorably linked with Wednesday Cricket Club from its very beginnings to the end of the nineteenth century and beyond. The association began on the first day of the cricket club when silver-plater William – born in Sheffield in 1791 – joined his five colleagues in founding the club. He was the club's first president, although it is not known how long he held office for; it is known that he was re-elected over thirty years later, serving between 1851 and 1856, before passing away early in 1859.

William was blessed with a total of seven children, and his eldest, Henry, was a member of the cricket club for an astonishing period of over fifty years. He followed his father into the silver-plating business – employing fifty workers in 1881 – and in the late 1880s also followed in his father's footsteps by being elected President of the Cricket Club. Two of Henry's sons, Sydney and Charles, were also involved in both the football and cricket sides of Wednesday, with Sydney serving as secretary for the summer game in the mid-1870s and also playing football, in addition to serving on the winter sport committee. His sibling, Charles, was mainly involved on the football side and was in the Wednesday side that won the Wharncliffe Charity Cup in 1879; he also appeared in FA Cup football.

The following season opened in May 1832 with the usual practice game and dinner at the Hyde Park Ground, with the evening 'passing with harmony and conviviality, as expected at such gatherings of admirers of the most "manly" sport'. The opening game of the summer of 1833 was worthy of note as the members played an inter-club game with surnames A–K facing L–Z, the former accruing a handsome 324 runs, from two innings, and latter just 133 – it was common in those days for innings scores to be well under 100, mainly due to the poor quality of outfields, so such high scoring would certainly have been a rarity. Wednesday also played the Friday Club later in the season, while the 1834 campaign started early with the members gathering at Hyde Park on the first Wednesday in April. A few weeks later an inter-club game saw the added attraction of Mr Green descending onto the Hyde Park pitch in a balloon, much to the delight of all in attendance.

The season ended with a representative game as ten of Yorkshire plus Tom Marsden faced ten of Wednesday CC plus Mr Collett (considered the best bowler in England at that time). The MCC member was in Sheffield for a week to give lessons to aspiring young bowlers, and he led Wednesday to victory. The summer of 1835 saw Wednesday play a twelve-a-side inter-club fixture while they met a team from Hull for the first time, the local bookies making the home side strong favourites despite the unknown opposition. The pre-match betting proved correct as, in front of a respectable Hyde Park crowd, Wednesday won by 39 runs after amassing 185 in their two innings. Two meetings with Chesterfield Albion were both lost, prior to a reciprocal visit to East Yorkshire, which ended the campaign for Wednesday, with the club sending a mixed XI to the Hull Cricket Ground and the game being the first to be played at the new enclosure. Wednesday received a warm welcome from the hosts and ended the season with a 27-run victory.

THOMAS LINDLEY

It has proven virtually impossible to categorically state which Thomas
Lindley was a founder member of the cricket club, mainly due to a lack
of census and birth records from the early nineteenth century. However,
what little information is available does suggest that Thomas was born
around 1795/96 in Sheffield and worked as a fork manufacturer. In 1841
and 1851, he was living as a lodger, latterly with the Cheetham Family of
Brightside, and it seems he never married. The name of Thomas Lindley
appeared on the cricket club's committee rolls in the early 1840s, while
on 14 April 1857 it was recorded that cutler Thomas Lindley had passed
away, due to chronic bronchitis, in Sheffield at the age of sixty-one.

The summers of 1836 and 1837 saw Wednesday play home and away
games against Chesterfield, with the former year seeing a handsome
115-run victory in Derbyshire before a five-wicket loss back at Hyde Park
– a game which saw founder member John Southern in the home side,
but very poor fielding costing Wednesday dearly. Incidentally, a prominent
member of the club around this time was famous Sheffield resident Thomas
Jessop, who in his life was Mayor of Sheffield, Master Cutler and founder
of Jessop Hospital for women. Another founding father, George Dawson,
appeared in the loss at Chesterfield in June 1837, while the return game
proved controversial as a good crowd watched Wednesday bowl out
Chesterfield for only 50 before collapsing themselves for 36. The visitors
scored a further 59, but, as Wednesday chased the 74 needed to win, the
'away' umpire – who had been anything but impartial – controversially
gave Wednesday man Woodcock out, and fans flooded onto the pitch to
air their displeasure. All the players returned to the pavilion, and when
the pitch was cleared the home umpire took his position and waited for
play to recommence. However, all but two of the Chesterfield side had
left the ground and gone into town where, despite being tracked down by
Marsden, they refused to return. Wednesday duly claimed the 'stake money'
on the basis of having been ahead on the first innings. Two single versus
married games also took place in the summer of 1837, although the earlier
game saw the club short of members with only seven attached gentleman
reporting for duty; three friends were recruited to ensure a ten-a-side match
could go ahead.

GEORGE EDWARD DAWSON

Co-founder George Dawson was a self-employed manufacturer producing
razors from his Sheffield-based premises. In addition to his trade, it is
believed he was also, along with his wife Ann, the licensee of the Old
White Lion public house at No. 2 the Wicker. Born in Sheffield on 19
March 1799, George was actually a professional cricketer between 1827
and 1836, mainly appearing for Sheffield Cricket Club – the forerunner of
Yorkshire CCC. He is credited with eight first-class games in that period,
scoring 105 runs and taking seven wickets, and appeared in the game
versus Norfolk in 1833, which is generally regarded as the first Yorkshire
CCC match. Despite playing cricket for a living, he still played an active
part in Wednesday CC affairs, being twice president in the latter part of
the 1820s and serving on the committee into the early 1840s. He married
his nurse wife in 1829 and became father to two boys and two girls; he
sadly died at the young age of forty-four in Sheffield on 3 May 1843.

The club's status and reputation ensured Wednesday were often cast in the
'missionary' role, and this was the case in June 1838 when the new Victoria
Ground in Leeds was officially opened with a visit from the famous Sheffield
team. Unfortunately, despite the ground being newly constructed, the pitch
was in terrible condition and, in poor weather, the home side recorded a
33-run victory despite Wednesday including Reuben Hallam, Sampson and
Dawson. The return fixture took place a month later with both sides practising
on the outfield for an hour before the start. Wednesday amassed 188 in their
first knock and this proved decisive as the game ended with a comfortable
139-run win. Experienced club men Marsden and Dearman then stood in
the middle as a young Wednesday XI beat the Pickwick Club at Hyde Park
before Wednesday faced a combined team drawn from the Thursday and
Friday clubs. Incidentally, around this time it was noted in the club's minute
book that ground staff (glorified ball-boys) were paid 2s a day 'though if not
in attendance at two o'clock they shall receive just one'. It was also noted in
the club ledger that Charles Ward and Isaac Hattersley were each fined half a
crown for breaching rule IX – leaving a ball on the field after play.

The summer also saw a unique match played at Hyde Park where all the
players were sixty years or over, including sixty-year-old founder Hardesty.
The cricket season was frequently being stretched into October, and in
1838 Wednesday played three fixtures in the month, commencing with a
second visit to the Victoria Ground where fourteen of Leeds beat eleven
Wednesday men (including brothers, Henry, Thomas and George Reaney)

by 168 runs. A comfortable win over the Burton Union club followed at Hyde Park before the return fixture – a 42-run win at Burton – saw stumps drawn for another season.

JOHN SOUTHERN

Of the six men who founded the Wednesday Club, only John Southern remains a true mystery. The only Southern on record as being born in Sheffield in the eighteenth century (1770) would certainly have been too old – he was still playing in the 1830s – so the only points of reference available are two trade directories published in 1822 and 1838. Both of these list a John Southern trading in the town as an 'agent for the highways' from his Norfolk Row office. It is known that John Southern served as club president in 1830 and was still on the cricket club committee in 1841, but neither census or newspaper archives can produce any further information on a gentleman that will probably forever remain a mystery.

Entries in the club minutes for 1839 gave a rare glimpse into how Wednesday were run with trivial items, to modern eyes, resolving to enquire about purchasing three socks, not to exceed 4s each. It was also stated that if players were not present at 9.30 a.m. on the morning of a match they would have to forfeit 1s. The club was certainly run professionally and this was perhaps one of the reasons why they were judged, and remained so for many years, as the best and most popular cricket club in Sheffield. Wednesday was also not one to avoid a challenge as in July 1839 they announced they would play any town in Yorkshire for between 11 and 22 sovereigns a side, home and away.

TOM MARSDEN

To say Tom Marsden was a true legend of the game of cricket in Sheffield would do little justice to his true standing and the reverence in which he was held by his multitude of supporters. Born in the town on 12 September 1803 at Brocco Bank, Tom was often referred to as the 'Brocco lad' and can lay claim to be the greatest ever batsman to have represented Wednesday. He was first noted playing for Mosbrorough in 1823, but his fame went countrywide after he scored an astonishing 227 in an 1826 representative game, becoming only the second player to score a double hundred in a first-class game – six years after William Ward achieved the feat at Lords.

Tom spent eight hours at the crease, over three days, to amass the score and then grabbed six Nottinghamshire wickets – Marsden was also a very useful bowler – and achieved instant immortality thanks to a thirteen stanza poem that was written about his feats, entitled 'Glorious Tom'.

His fame was such that in May 1827, long before the days of any mass communication, he received a cricket bat, with his name upon it in gilt, from a totally unknown patron from London. In the same year, Tom scored 117 in a Sheffield versus Nottingham fixture, and a year later the carefree left-handed batsman recorded two more centuries to cement his place as one of the most eminent batsmen in the North of England. Between 1826 and 1834 he scored 806 runs in twenty completed innings, averaging just fewer than 40 runs per knock – an incredible average in those early days of organised cricket.

For the vast majority of the 1820s he was also the greatest single wicket cricketer in Northern England, and Tom – a man not short on confidence – publicly stated he would beat all-comers for £50 stake money. It was great Southern cricketer Fuller Pilch who eventually took his single wicket crown, with over 20,000 packing into the Darnall Grounds in 1828 to see Marsden lose heavily. The loss proved a blow for Tom, although he still retained his northern single wicket title until 1841 when fellow Wednesday man Sampson took his crown. In 1831, his Sheffield cricket friends presented him with an inscribed silver trophy, which would have cost an astonishing £4,500 today, while Tom became landlord of the Cricketers Inn, Darnall. He continued to aid Wednesday throughout the 1830s, coaching and playing for other sides in the early 1840s such as Denton and Leeds. Unfortunately for Tom, he became rather too fond of drinking with customers at his premises, and this excess contributed greatly to his eventual death at the age of thirty-nine from consumption on 27 February 1843. His funeral was attended by members of the Cricket Club and hundreds of his townsfolk, where a tribute said that Marsden 'was born in humble circumstances yet, by his integrity, he passed through life with an unsullied reputation'.

Despite his passing at such an early age, his name lived on with every subsequent Wednesday annual meeting including a toast to Tom from his Silver Cup, which had been presented back to Wednesday. In June 1850, friends of Tom also met at Mr Woollen's White Lion public house at Heeley to hand over a subscription to his only son, William, so he could be apprenticed to one of the staple trades in the town – founding member William Stratford organising the great show of benevolence. Even today – thanks to the reformed Wednesday CC – the deeds of Marsden live on as the splendid trophy was restored and is now competed for annually.

A New Decade as Wednesday
Stretch Their Wings

The season of 1840 opened at Hyde Park with a win for the married players against the singletons before Manchester-based Denton visited Sheffield to face Wednesday, to whose name was now being consistently added the prefix of Sheffield. The home club was described as 'those staunch and almost only supporters of the manly and truly English game of cricket in this town', and it was Wednesday who comfortably won despite the away side being aided by 'Old Tom' (Marsden) who disappointed his fans by only getting 6 in the first innings before showing some of his old form to top score with 32 in Denton's second knock.

THOMAS HUNT

Born in Chesterfield in 1819, Tom Hunt represented Wednesday during the 1840s, having started his cricket career with the side that represented the Derbyshire town – Hunt appearing for Chesterfield against Wednesday in July 1843. Hunt was an outstanding batsman and is said to have won more single-wicket matches than any other cricketer – his 165 total against George Chatterton in 1843 was also a record for that format of the game. He was first noted in Wednesday whites at the commencement of the 1844 season when he captained one of two chosen twelve-man teams, scoring 15 runs. At the end of that summer he showed his qualities by scoring 55 runs and taking five wickets as Wednesday beat the Royds Mill Club.

A coach-maker by trade, Tom was a professional cricketer between 1844 and 1858, appearing for Sheffield Cricket Club before moving across the Pennines to begin an engagement at Manchester CC in 1851, which lasted seven years. During that time he represented the All England XI (a forerunner of the National side) on several occasions, but his story had a tragic end. On 11 September 1858 he had been playing in an eleven of England versus twenty of Rochdale in the Lancashire town, when, in order to catch his train back to Manchester, he cut across the train tracks – as he had done on many occasions. The decision proved fatal; he became trapped as the 7.00 p.m. passed the cricket ground, and was helpless as the train ran over him, severing both his legs at the calves and shattering one hand. He was carried from the tracks and his wife was called for, but, tragically, 5 minutes before she arrived, he passed away, aged just thirty-nine. He left a widow and four children, and various benefit games were staged in his honour after the terrible event.

The game of cricket had become the nation's favourite sport and although mainly played in the summer months, fans of the game in Sheffield were also treated to the phenomenon that was 'cricket on ice'. The games – first recorded in January 1826 – tended to be held on frozen lakes and saw all the players wear skates to help them manoeuvre around the 'pitch'. A display of fireworks usually preceded the start and this was the case on 8 February 1841, when Mr Gascoyne's pyrotechnics preceded two representative sides meeting at the Little London Dam in Heeley.

The stumps were 'pitched' at 12 noon and hundreds watched a game that entered into Sheffield sporting folklore due to the amazing feat of Harry Sampson who hit 162 – the highest ever score on ice. His side, which also included Wednesday men Henry Wilson and Richard Gillott, amassed over 300 runs in their innings, with their opponents losing their first four wickets for only 8 runs before darkness prevented further play. Another display of fireworks ended the day's entertainment before all the players retired to the Union Inn, run by Wednesday cricketer Henry Bolsover, for a sumptuous supper. It was also noted in 1841 that Wednesday had six bats waiting to be repaired and had committed to purchasing two new ones – one at 3s 6d and one at 4s.

JAMES DEARMAN

Sheffield-born on 7 December 1807, James Dearman was another of the outstanding cricketers to emerge from the town in the 1830s. Known as 'Jem' or 'Little Jim' to his friends, he first came to prominence in single wicket cricket, although in September 1833 he scored a total of 54 runs and took three wickets as a side playing under the umbrella of Yorkshire met Norfolk at Hyde Park CG. A comprehensive single-wicket win over Nottingham club player Tom Heath in October 1833 led Dearman to challenge anyone in the country to back him for £50 against all comers. His crown slipped in August 1838 when the MCC arranged a single-wicket game in Sheffield against the celebrated Kent cricketer Alfred Mynn, which Dearman lost comprehensively. As well as appearing for Wednesday CC, he was also a regular for Sheffield CC, but sadly, like so many of his contemporaries, he died at an early age, taken by Asiatic cholera at his Darnall home on 3 September 1854 aged forty-seven. He left a widow and nine children, and his cricket friends arranged a subscription on behalf his near destitute family.

In April 1842 Wednesday staged their first Cricket Ball, held at Hyde Park House, where the arrangements 'delighted the company and the evening passed in the most agreeable manner', although the event was seemingly not repeated. Just under a month later the opening practice game took place at Hyde Park, accompanied by the usual post-match dinner, provided this time by the new proprietor of the ground, Mr Hyde. The players and their friends duly enjoyed an evening of 'harmony, hilarity and good feeling' to launch the club's twenty-second season. The game at Dalton Magna CC in June 1842 proved highly controversial as both sides strained to win the £40 stake money. The teams were relatively close after the first innings, and the home side were eventually chasing 63 to win. However, wickets quickly tumbled and with the score at 14-4, the hosts disputed a decision from the umpire and refused to continue. After a half hour delay, the umpire awarded the game to Wednesday, although Dalton refused to hand over their stake money with Wednesday accusing them of 'violating the principles of honour, equality and truth'. In August 1842, the cricket club enjoyed a grand day out in Chatsworth Park where they faced a combined side drawn from local clubs Chatsworth, Pillsby, Edensor and Curbage. The selected XI, coached by veteran Marsden, won by two wickets before the local MP captained a side against an eleven led by the 6th Duke of Chatsworth's head gardener! The season ended with a match against Dalton – promoted as the 'Championship of Yorkshire' by new Hyde Park proprietor Mr J. Holland – and it would prove to be the final appearance of Marsden in Wednesday whites. He delighted his fans with some great stroke play, as Wednesday won the £100 stake money, but he was clearly unwell and would not survive the oncoming winter. An insight into the club's relationship with the landlord of the Hyde Park ground (as opposed to the proprietor, who was involved in the day-to-day running of the venue) was revealed in 1843, with Sam Heathcote receiving an annual rent of £12 for use of the ground on every Wednesday throughout the season. Wednesday were also entitled to practice on any other day, free of expense, and all members allowed admission at all times. The Landlord would have first preference of managing games, paying all expenses and receiving all gate monies, while if he refused, Wednesday were at liberty to organise said games.

SAMUEL WRIGHT

Although no contemporary evidence exists, it is believed (though purely anecdotal) that Sam Wright was a member of the Wednesday Cricket Club in the 1830s before setting sail for a new life in the Americas. Sam, along with his wife Anne and son Harry, is certainly recorded as arriving on US shores in the summer of 1836. Little is known of Sheffield-born Sam's early life, although the fact that he graduated from Balliol College, part of Oxford University, suggests that he came from a privileged background. In Sheffield he worked as a wood turner, while 'over the pond' he became a professional cricketer for (the fantastically named) New York-based St George Dragonslayers Cricket Club in 1837. He would captain the club for an astonishing thirty-three years before taking over in 1857 as groundskeeper and general factotum – a person who has many diverse activities or responsibilities.

He played for America in the first ever international cricket match, against Canada in the 'Big Apple' in September 1844, and took five wickets in a game that drew a 20,000-strong crowd and saw $120,000 wagered on the result. The mid-nineteenth century was a boom time for the sport in North America, before the Civil War brought an end to its growth. It was effectively replaced by the sport of baseball, and incredibly it was Sam's Sheffield-born son, Harry, who is now recognised as the 'father of baseball' as he was without doubt the most influential figure in the sport in those early years as it emerged as the national sport of the US.

The new season opened in early May 1843 with the now usual inter-club practice game and opening dinner. The top scorer was John Smith, with 48, and members later enjoyed dinner provided by Mr Holland; after the cloth was drawn they sang party songs of glee and toasted various worthies. The first club game of the summer resulted in a 77-run win at Chesterfield. John Smith scored a century two weeks later and was one of the four 'players' assisting 'seven gentleman' as the select side beat Wednesday by over an innings, with Michael Ellison also notching a 'considerable' total as Wednesday's opponents scored close to 300, which was a winning tally in the mid-1840s. The old club, described as 'the best supporters of cricket in the town', opened the following season on Wednesday 1 May 1844 when a side captained by Ward faced twelve men led by Hunt. Soon after, the married men won again, while a junior side beat Stannington by 61 runs. The summer of 1844 was indeed a busy one as several more games were still to be played, the season stretching into mid-October once more. Fixtures included a Hyde Park game against the Hyston Green CC of Nottingham, although the visiting side was bolstered significantly by some of the better players of Nottinghamshire. Wednesday lost only narrowly before a single-run victory at Chesterfield that meant that the visitors walked away with the prize on offer – a new cricket ball. The emerging talent of all-rounder Hunt was clearly shown in the final game: scoring 55 and grabbing five wickets as his side narrowly beat a team consisting of ten men of the Royds Mill CC plus All England batsman William Lillywhite.

WILLIAM SLINN

William Slinn was born in Sheffield on 13 December 1826 and became one of the greatest fast bowlers of his generation, appearing in nineteen first-class games and taking 111 wickets at an average of 13.20 runs – his best bowling figures being 8 for 33 against Surrey. An overarm, right-handed bowler, William was hailed as the 'straightest' bowler in England and represented Yorkshire CCC in 1864 as well as playing for the White Rose in pre-county days. In the days before the England cricket team, he appeared for various select sides including the All England XI, United England XI and North of England, while his most remarkable feat came against the first named in 1862 when he took all ten second innings wickets for 32 runs while playing for a select XI. He was, however, the archetypical No. 11 as he amassed only 46 first-class runs at an average of just two. In Sheffield cricket he was only ever associated with Wednesday, serving on the committee (1852–55), and was a regular for the club throughout the 1850s as well as playing for Wednesday in the two decades that followed; he also appeared in the first match played at Bramall Lane. He was held in such high esteem by his Sheffield friends that an All England XI versus eighteen of Sheffield match was organised in 1863 for his benefit.

Throughout his working life, Slinn was primarily employed as a cricket professional, although he did work in Sheffield in the 1840s as a scissor grinder. As a professional player he also represented Burnley CC, and he was also a highly regarded coach, working at Oxford University (1859–70) and Cambridge University (1870–86) while also coaching for such prestigious academia as Winchester and Harrow schools. William was still playing in his hometown in the early 1880s, but passed away on 17 June 1888, aged sixty-one, at his residence on Harrington Road, Highfields.

The club's silver jubilee season proved a disappointment as Wednesday seemingly played only a handful of games, and this was reflected at the opening match of the 1846 season when members, dining at Sam Heathcote's Inn, were of the opinion that 'the game of cricket would greatly revive in the town'. The other 'significant' club in the town, Sheffield CC, were subsequently beaten at Hyde Park before the club's junior side were again in action, enjoying a pleasant day trip to face Baslow. The biggest game of the summer though involved several Wednesday players, who appeared for the twenty-two against eleven of All England in September 1846. The match was played for the 200 gold sovereigns and created huge interest in the town with around 2,000 fans paying sixpence – double the usual price – to toll collectors at the Hyde Park entrance gate on day one. A large tent was also erected on the ground, pitched on the sloping part of the enclosure, and Mr Heathcote's Inn was crammed to excess. Brick booths sold cuts of beef and ham and barrels of porter (a dark beer) and ale kept the spectators refreshed. The England XI scored 80 and 106 in their two innings, but it was Wednesday stalwart Sampson who hit the winning run as the home side took the considerable pot with five wickets to spare. Around 12,000 people attended the three-day game and emphatically showed that the appetite for cricket in Sheffield had not diminished. Another stake match – for £50 – ended the season with the local press surprised that Broomhall has 'dared' to challenge the 'old Wednesday club', which it was considered had all Sheffield's best players. It was therefore a huge shock when a young opposition side comprehensively beat Wednesday – by an innings and 44 runs.

MICHAEL ELLISON

Michael Ellison was first noted as secretary and treasurer of Lead Works Cricket Club in the late 1830s. Ellison, born 1 June 1817 in Worksop, would later be involved with Sheffield CC, around 1843, and would be an active player and member of Wednesday CC. He went on to play sixteen first-class games between 1846 and 1855, scoring 195 runs and securing one wicket, and was held in such high esteem in Sheffield cricket circles that in March 1851 he was presented with an elegant candelabrum at a gala dinner attended by the Lord Mayor. The item was made by Sheffield silversmiths Hawksworth & Eyre and was inscribed with 'presented to Michael Joseph Ellison Esq, by his fellow townsmen, admirers of cricket, for his persevering and generous exertions in promoting that manly and national game in the town of Sheffield'.

Ellison is, however, remembered more for his deeds off the field of play as he was instrumental in the building and management of Bramall Lane and the formation of Yorkshire County Cricket Club – he served as president from 1864–97. He followed in the footsteps of his father, as the Sheffield agent to the Duke of Norfolk, and although not a great supporter of football, he served Sheffield United FC as President between 1891 until his death, aged eighty-one, on 12 July 1898 at Broomhall, Sheffield.

The opening game of the 1847 season saw selected sides that included George Chatterton (no relation of Benjamin) and Gillott, while Wednesday reiterated their status in the town by defeating Sheffield CC. Eleven played eighteen in the final game of the summer – to ensure all of the club members were involved – while the now annual meeting, in April 1848, was held at the abode of John Barker, publican of the Thatched House Tavern, High Street. It was reported by the secretary that the prospect of the club, both financially and otherwise, was most cheering and that play would commence in early May. The season duly started at Hyde Park, which had been greatly improved over the winter months with the sloping side of the ground raised so the racecourse could be seen from all around the ground, and a considerable number of trees planted, greatly adding to the beauty of the enclosure. The two sides were picked by Secretary Francis Hawke and included the likes of Sampson, Chatterton (George and Ben), William Smith and Gillott, although the cricket correspondent of the *Sheffield Independent* condemned the fielding. A relatively rare visit to the Royds Ground, home of Sheffield CC, was next with the teams involved in a thrilling encounter – described as one of the greatest matches ever seen in Sheffield – which was eventually drawn.

A few weeks later, cricket proved it also had its charitable side as a game took place for the benefit of the Sheffield Infirmary, with Sampson the major protagonist behind the match. It was clear that in the early years of the cricket club's history, the game not only provided its members with a healthy and enjoyable sport, in a town that was becoming increasingly industrialised and polluted, but also served as a great social outlet from which life-long friendships were born. This could not be more exemplified than in August 1848, when Wednesday travelled to Chatsworth Park on a summer's afternoon. The match took place during 'Wake's Week' (a period when all the factories, collieries and industries closed) and the whole club seemed to travel into Derbyshire, despite Wednesday fielding a relatively young side against a Baslow XI. It was noted that even a sprinkling of ladies attended the fixture, and there were huge cheers from the crowd when the Duke of Devonshire passed by in his carriage to take his seat. The home side took the honours before the whole party retired to the Wheat Sheaf Inn, situated in the grounds, with several having found partners among the 'bright eyed maidens' of Baslow. The players and friends duly 'tripped the light fantastic toe', dancing and taking refreshment late into the night.

HENRY SAMPSON

Sheffield-born on 13 March 1813, Henry Sampson was one of the finest cricketers of his generation and a much-loved member of the Sheffield sporting scene. A file forger initially employed at Cammell & Johnson on Furnival Street, he first came to be noticed on the cricket field in July 1832 when he competed in a single-wicket match at Hyde Park. Until 1840 he played for Wednesday and Sheffield, with his best display for the former being an aggregate score of 57, in a match against Denton in June 1840. In the same year he twice appeared for the North of England versus MCC, and a year later was contracted as a ground bowler for the latter. He was now at the peak of his game, and after playing in a Gentleman v Players match at Lords in 1841 he returned home to take the single-wicket crown from Tom Marsden – winning by an innings and 50 runs.

Earlier in the year he had scored the highest ever total, 162, recorded in cricket played on ice. He was subsequently employed for two years as a professional by Reading CC, also taking a public house in the town before returning to Sheffield in 1845, becoming the landlord of the Crown and Anchor Inn. He remained there until September 1848 when he moved to the Adelphi Hotel on Arundel Street. In December 1848 he had received a huge sterling silver tankard from fellow townsfolk as a testimonial to his talents and popularity. His new abode became the hub for all cricketers in Sheffield, with Wednesday holding all their AGMs at the hotel from the early 1850s onwards. During his early years as a licensee, 5-foot 4-inches-tall Henry continued to play cricket to a high standard, appearing for All England versus Kent at Lords in July 1851, and became a regular for the club bearing the Adelphi's name. He finally retired as a professional around 1857 and later joined the Yorkshire CCC committee while his hotel was a regular haunt for visiting teams who faced Yorkshire at Bramall Lane. After almost twenty years at the Adelphi, he retired in April 1868, although he continued to be actively involved in every facet of Sheffield cricket.

A widower, Henry suffered a short but severe illness, which resulted in a paralytic stroke; he passed away at his Broomhall home on 29 March 1885, aged seventy-two. His success on the cricket field ensured his son George received an excellent education, becoming an architect and surveyor as well as playing regularly for Wednesday FC throughout the 1870s.

It was reported at the 1849 opening game that the club had been on the wane the previous summer, but was 'expected to be very numerous and powerful thro the exertions of some old members', although the twelve bottles of wine, kindly provided by Mr Heathcote, no doubt contributed to the positive vibes emanating from the meeting. Late in the season, Wednesday made a maiden visit to Balbrough where fans came from all the neighbouring villages to watch the game with the visiting XI winning comfortably. In early July, Wednesday visited Glossop for the first time – a fixture that would become a permanent feature of the club's summer. Wednesday fielded their 3rd XI, but underestimated their new opponents as the Derbyshire club took the honours. Wednesday made a second visit late in the season, winning by 41 runs, with the fixture being treated as a senior game from that day forward.

Sheffield Gets a New Cricket Ground

The new decade commenced at Hyde Park in April 1850, with the usual practice game and dinner with a 10s subscription required to join the club ranks, which would guarantee admission to all cricket games held at the ground. Home and away games were duly played against Glossop, while cricket in the town was generally booming – several games being played every weekend. New opponents for Wednesday included the Regent Club – beaten by four wickets with Gillott impressing with an unbeaten 38 – and the Skating Club, who lost heavily after Wednesday amassed 225 in their first innings. The April 1851 AGM saw departing secretary Francis Hawke presented with a silver-plated liqueur frame (akin to a wine rack) as a thank you for his five years of service – a new position on the Duke of Norfolk's Glossop estate being the reason for his resignation. Wednesday played ten matches in the 1851 season, against the likes of Worksop, Rotherham and Sheffield, and the campaign was such a success that the club was able to carry a large cash surplus forward.

JOHN BERRY

It is believed that John Berry was the first professional employed by Wednesday, being contracted between 1851 and 1861. It was, however, not an exclusive contract as, in the same era, Berry received remuneration to appear for Sheffield, Rotherham and Carlisle clubs. Born in Huddersfield on 10 January 1823, Berry worked for many years as the personal servant to Michael Ellison while also appearing eighteen times for Yorkshire CCC, scoring 1,069 runs and taking forty wickets. A right-handed batsman and medium-pace bowler, Berry, who earned the nickname of 'honest John', also appeared for Yorkshire when they were a pre-county club and represented England and the North on several occasions. He eventually moved across the Pennines to settle in Lancashire, being employed as a professional at Accrington. He was still playing in the late 1860s – scoring 135 for Accrington against Todmorden in July 1867 – and passed away on 26 February 1895, aged seventy-two, in Haslingden.

The 1852 summer saw Wednesday face the Sheffield-based Athenaeum Club for the first time, with a side containing Ben Chatterton, Slinn and George Skinner securing a narrow victory. The following season opened at Hyde Park, with sides selected by Berry and Gillott who met prior to the usual opening dinner. A low scoring game – the combined totals accruing less than 100 runs – saw Berry comfortably top score with 29, although the excellent bowling of Berry and Slinn was a contributory factor in the miserly scores. A first meeting with Eckington followed, and it was presentation time again when retiring Secretary Joseph Lockwood received a 'handsome' tea and coffee service in appreciation of his services, before the members sat down to another excellent supper provided by Mrs Heathcote. The club's time at Hyde Park was coming to a close; a public meeting on 30 January 1854 would mark the beginning of the end for Sheffield's second great cricket arena. The Hyde Park ground had slowly started to deteriorate from the early 1850s onwards, and there was much debate among the Sheffield cricketing fraternity discussing what could be done about its sad decline. A new ground at Newhall was briefly used but was considered too far from town and boasted a sub-standard wicket. Therefore, members of the Sheffield CC – and all the major clubs of the town – met at the Adelphi to hear a proposal from Michael Ellison with regard to a new ground. The meeting was asked to consider an offer from the Duke of Norfolk regarding the appropriation of a piece of land for the purpose of a new public ground. His grace had offered a ninety-nine-year lease on a 9-acre plot of land by Bramall Lane, with a yearly rent of £5 per acre and a gentleman's agreement that it would only be used for sporting purposes. Ellison's position as agent to the Duke was a major factor in the offer, and Wednesday 'kingpin' William Stratford proposed that it should be accepted – fellow SWCC member Thomas Linley seconding. Stratford commented that cricketers had 'nothing to fear' and that Wednesday 'had grown tired of suffering the inconvenience of playing first rate matches on grounds totally unsuited to the display of cricket talent'. A committee was duly formed, containing representatives from Sheffield, Athenaeum, Adelphi, Milton, Wednesday, Exchange and Bowling clubs. The Sheffield United Cricket and Bowling Club was subsequently formed to oversee the building and management of the proposed new ground, although the body did not actually have any players or play any games. A £5 subscription was quickly opened and most of the required monies were raised by the end of the year.

What would be Wednesday's final season at Hyde Park commenced in May 1854, for which 10s subscriptions were available from Sampson at the Adelphi. The break from Hyde Park was confirmed in March 1855 when members at the club's AGM voted unanimously to discontinue playing at the venue and arrange for use of the soon to be opened Bramall Lane. The meeting also reported that the club's finances were still in a healthy state with the £11 in the bank account worth considerably more than today's value. The big day finally arrived on 30 April 1855 when Sheffield, Wednesday, Broomhall, Milton, Caxton and Shrewsbury – the six clubs who had negotiated to use Bramall Lane – picked sides for The Eleven versus The Twenty-Two. The ground was not quite completed, but when finished it ranked inferior to none, boasting ample platforms on the 'exclusive' side of the ground while on the opposite side – John Street - a building was erected, the lower four compartments of which were occupied by publicans – Donoghue's being best known. The upper part consisted of a covered gallery for spectators while low wooden sheds acted as dressing rooms. The opening game featured Wednesday men Ben Chatterton, Hallam, Gillott and Sampson, and after two days' play the game finished, rather fittingly, in a draw.

GEORGE ULYETT

Born in Pitsmoor, Sheffield, on 21 October 1851, George Ulyett was arguably the most famous man to appear for both cricket and football sections. He played in a solitary FA Cup tie in 1883 for Wednesday FC, but was better known for his deeds on the cricket square. He was regarded as the greatest Yorkshire cricketer of the nineteenth century, scoring over 1,000 runs in a season on ten occasions, and was capped twenty-five times by England. His top score for the Tykes came in 1887 when he recorded 199 at Bramall Lane against Derbyshire. He appeared for his country in the first ever test match, against Australia in 1877, and is famed for a moment at Lord's against the Aussies in 1884 when he somehow caught and bowled hard hitter George Bonner to the amazement of the crowd. Cricket legend W.G. Grace later wrote in his memoirs that he thought him 'foolish' to even attempt the catch as he believed he would have suffered a broken arm if the attempt had been mistimed. He remained an amateur throughout his career – working in the Sheffield steel industry as a sheet roller – although he ceased playing football in 1883 because of injury. Sadly he died young of pneumonia, aged just forty-seven, on 18 June 1898 at the Pine Hotel, Pitsmoor, after watching his beloved Yorkshire CCC play Kent at Bramall Lane.

The first Wednesday game played at their new home came nine days later when a Sampson XI beat a Wright XI by 72 runs, William Walton top scoring with 46. Home and away games were also played against Glossop while on a sunny day in August 1855 the club, totalling around sixty members, travelled en masse to Baslow for an inter-club game. Heavy rain caused the cancellation of the opening game of the 1856 season, although the opening dinner – with new secretary Thomas Frith in attendance – still went ahead. It was stated that Wednesday were believed to be the oldest provincial club in England, but it was a season of frustration as a rainy summer meant many matches were lost, including against Glossop (twice) and Sheffield. Games were played against the newly formed Mechanics Club while the 'old style' sweepstakes ties underwent a bit of revival, with Wednesday taking the £50 pot against Milton. They duly qualified for the final against Hallam and won a thrilling game by a solitary run.

The match proved controversial as Hallam was left disgruntled by some decisions of the umpire, believing he had denied them the win. The local press said 'it is a great pity, but a notorious fact, that almost on every occasion when a cricket match is played for money the losing party never give in without questioning the correctness of the decision of the umpire'. It would be many years though before the high stakes games were confined to the history books, Wednesday last being involved for £60 versus Lacelies Hall in 1867, with teams then just playing for a ball (1868–78) and then just for the love of the game. Meanwhile the season ended as it had started with poor weather, although the handful of members that did assemble heartily tucked into Mrs Sampson's delicious supper. Wednesday did manage to complete ten games in the season, winning six and losing two.

Despite the poor weather of 1856, Wednesday were in 'rude' health with membership increasing by thirty to eighty-six members for the 1857 season, and twenty generously offered to double their subscriptions to give players the opportunity to play matches further afield. Over forty gentlemen sat down to the opening dinner in May 1857, with Gillott presiding, and Wednesday would experience a busy summer with a highlight being a game in Chatsworth Park against a local XI. Star performer William Slinn grabbed five wickets in a win at Newark, while the strength of the club was shown by the staging of several junior games. The club managed to lose both of their sweepstake matches against Milton and Broomhall, and were forced to settle for a draw in a two-day Bramall Lane game when Newark had to leave early to catch the train home. By the time of the closing game, membership had climbed to a record 103 and Wednesday had played a total of 17 games. A profit had also been recorded on the season, despite increased costs, resulting in the committee deciding to offer five trophies for the best batters and bowlers.

JOHN TASKER

John Tasker was without doubt one of the major figures in Victorian Sheffield as he not only served the corporation for twenty years – standing as Lord Mayor in the mid-1870s – but was also a pioneer of the use of the telephone and electricity in the town. Born around 1817 in Sheffield, Tasker's main business was actually as a footwear manufacturer, but he eventually diversified into various trades including patenting an armour plate grinding machine, which at one point was responsible for making all the armour plating on the British Navy's ships. His motto was 'adaptability'; he produced items such as a bouncy rubber ball and a way of mending galoshes using Indian rubber. It was, however, his involvement with the telephone for which he became best known. He was intrigued by the device when it arrived in England and it duly prompted him to open Sheffield's first telephone exchange, which boasted just twelve initial subscribers. His business also helped build Sheffield's first power station and electricity supply network. Messers Tasker & Sons were behind the famous first football match lit by electric light in 1878.

In addition to all of his worthy contributions to Sheffield, Tasker was also a keen lover of local sport and was associated with Wednesday cricket club for many years. He was secretary between 1856 and 1859 and served on the committee throughout the rest of the decade. In later life he worked as admissions officer and accountant at the Ecclesshall Bierlow Union Workhouse and lived his final days in the leafy suburb of Fulwood. He never recovered from the blow of losing his wife, Jane, and just eleven weeks after her passing, died on 18 April 1877, aged sixty. The family name continued with his son William, who was involved with Wednesday CC for many years, serving as President between 1889 and 1891. Tasker's original company, now called Tasker UK Limited, continues to trade today.

The 1858 season saw a first meeting with Nottingham Commercial, Wednesday amassing a score of 237 despite four men being out for a duck, while Slinn continued to impress as he was presented with the best bowler award at the annual dinner. The April 1859 AGM resulted in the election of Skinner to the role of secretary, replacing the outgoing Tasker. Wednesday showed their ambition by requesting games with several clubs, including Gainsborough, Elsecar, Milton, Regent and United Mechanics. Wednesday would win four and lose four of eleven games played with the likes of Staveley and Hoyland met for the first time, the latter game being won convincingly when the hosts only amassed a total of 45 in their two innings. Wednesday included John Rodgers Snr and Jnr in that win at Hoyland, and, at the end of season awards, the older member of the Rodgers family duly presented the best cricketer trophy to John Berry. That closing dinner marked the end of the 1850s. Little did those members know that by the time another decade had passed the landscape of the Sheffield sporting scene would be almost unrecognisable. Before those changes, Wednesday welcomed in the new decade with an opening game at Bramall Lane, which was drawn, before losing both 1st XI and 2nd XI matches to Sheffield Collegiate School.

A total of twelve games were played in 1860 with the end of season meeting doubling as a presentation night to President Gillott, who received an electroplated tea and coffee service manufactured by acclaimed local firm Martin Hall & Co. with the inscription 'presented to Mr Richard Gillott, by members of the Sheffield Wednesday Cricket Club, as a token of esteem for his valuable service during a series of years Nov. 21st 1860'. Meanwhile, the early years of Bramall Lane had seen the management committee struggle to cover even the basic maintenance costs, and it was Ellison who had to fulfil his undeclared promise to pay the annual rent from his own pocket. Despite those financial problems, the venue had become a much loved home for Sheffield cricket, and two of the tenants, Wednesday and Shrewsbury, met there in June 1861. Opponents Shrewsbury broke up around 1892 and it was a Wednesday side, including Henry Bocking, who opened the new season with a victory. The 1861 campaign would not be a vintage one for Sheffield cricket in general, subscriptions to all clubs having fallen off somewhat due to the depressed state of Sheffield trade, but Wednesday continued to face more new clubs such as Elsecar and played fifteen matches in total, eight of which were classified as 'first-class' fixtures. A second team game, against York, was actually played at Endcliffe while the bowling prize went to James Dignum. The opening match and dinner in the 1862 campaign saw the 'Marsden Cup' filled to the brim with 'good old port' and heartily drunk from, and various toasts included the usual to the original benefactor. A subsequent game against Shrewsbury at Bramall

Lane provided a somewhat fortuitous two-wicket win for Wednesday as consequence of the umpire's watch being a few minutes slow – the match actually ended in a draw at the correct time. A few days later, Wednesday met the Riddings Club – based at Pye Bridge, Alfreton – and claimed a narrow victory after stumps were drawn just before the home team could secure the 8 runs needed. It proved another busy season for Wednesday with trips to Scarborough and a much more local game at Pitsmoor. Wednesday also paid the greatly anticipated visit to Glossop, where the spectators were treated to a thrilling game. Wednesday won by just 3 runs when Gillott made a superb catch at cover point to clinch the victory. In contrast to previous seasons, the club's final game of the campaign – at Bramall Lane in October 1862 – was not followed by the closing dinner, which was held a month later at the Adelphi. Among the prize winners were Thomas Brownhill and Bocking (best batters), Charley Hill (best 1st XI player) and Thomas Anderson (best 2nd and 3rd XI bowler).

RICHARD GILLOTT

Sheffield born in 1823, Richard Gillott was one of the greatest figures in the cricket club's history. His father, Samuel, left home at a young age to fight under the Duke of Wellington in the 1807–14 Peninsular War and Richard would follow his father into the trade of file grinding. A man of great presence and personality, he was also deeply religious, worshipping regularly at St Mary's church in Bramall Lane. He first became involved with Wednesday in the early 1840s and is recorded as being club president as early as 1848. He also served in the role between 1857 and 1863 and played virtually his whole career with Wednesday. He was one of the original shareholders of the Bramall Lane Cricket Ground and played in the first game, top scoring for his side with 19 runs before being caught by Sampson. He led the Wednesday batting averages in several seasons and remained an active member for three decades. Away from cricket he was recognised as one of the finest skaters in England and was at one time President of the Sheffield Skating Club. His son Joseph followed in his dad's footsteps as both President of the skating club and great social favourite. He was also a renowned musical composer. Richard Gillott was still working at the turn of the century after being widowed in the late 1890s, but survived only a few more months before passing away at his Meersbrook Park Road home aged seventy-eight on 2 December 1901.

The following year was significant for a meeting at the Adelphi on 25 April 1863, when Michael Ellison proposed the 'formation of a County Cricket club with its object to provide funds for the playing of first-class county matches, either in Sheffield or in other towns of the county, according as arrangement may be made', the motion was agreed and Yorkshire CCC was born with Sheffield Lord Mayor Thomas Barker (who was also a Wednesday patron) appointed the first President, and Ellison treasurer. Included on that first committee were Wednesday men Hawksley, Sampson and Gillott, while in club cricket it was the busiest season yet with a wide variety of games played as Wednesday fielded three teams.

The club won sixteen of the twenty-three games played, with highlights including a bowling hat-trick and 36 runs for John Rodgers in an easy win against Sheffield Collegiate and a terrific individual knock of 102 by Thomas Brownhill in a win over the Garrison club. In a break from tradition, the closing match was played on a handicap basis where players were penalised, in sporting parlance, according to the number of runs they'd obtained in the season. Wednesday were on such an upward curve that at that opening dinner of 1864, they even announced their hopes of attracting an All England XI to Bramall Lane, although this did not come to fruition. Membership was available from secretary Anderson at his corn exchange office, and with numbers booming – thirty signing up in one month – the most popular club in the town enjoyed another busy summer with new opponents including Knaresborough, Tapton and Howard Hill CC plus the usual games against Glossop and Collegiate, Thorpe claiming wickets in four consecutive balls as he recorded figures of 6-8 against the latter. The club's AGM continued to be held at Sampson's Adelphi, while it was reported that, due to increasing membership (125 in 1864 to 145 in 1865) the club had decided to take an extra wicket at Bramall Lane on both Wednesday and Saturday, with membership set at 12s, 6d. Future football club mainstay John Marsh was appointed assistant secretary in August 1865.

Wednesday felt aggrieved in a game against Chatsworth when batsman Earnshaw was given out by the umpire while he was still taking his position at the wicket and adjusting his glasses. At the closing dinner of 1865 the club welcomed the American Consul, Mr Abbott. It was stated that Wednesday had contributed the greatest number of professionals to the cricket world. The club played twenty-four matches in the summer, although it was reported that problems had arisen due to apathy shown by several of the better players – other clubs encountered the same issue – and it had often been difficult to field a really good side. A total of 2,216 runs were scored with Marsh appearing in the most games and Anderson the best bowler.

TOM ARMITAGE

Wednesday and Yorkshire CCC player Tom Armitage was born in Walkley, Sheffield, on 25 April 1848 and holds the distinction of being the first player to be capped at Test level by England – his surname ensuring that he was, alphabetically, number one in the order of caps when appearing in the Test match against Australia in Melbourne in March 1877. He was only capped twice by his country, scoring 33 runs and bowling only 12 balls, but spent six summers with the White Rose County before emigrating to the United States in 1879. He played the last of his fifty-seven first-class games in the US and passed away in Chicago, aged seventy-four on 21 September 1922. The family name lived on however as two of his grandsons, Tom and Len, played professional football for Wednesday FC – the latter appearing for the football club in the 1919/20 season. The story has a sad ending as on Christmas Eve 1923 Tom Jnr collapsed while playing in a reserve game for Wednesday. He was taken to hospital, but passed away five days later aged just twenty-four, which tragically ended the Armitage association with Wednesday.

A Gillott versus Anderson club game opened the 1866 season. Although membership had fallen back to 120, the club still ran three sides, with the highlight being figures of 8-17 by John Rodgers, against Barnsley Locke. Those figures were almost beaten when Barber recorded 7-15, versus Handsworth Woodhouse, as Wednesday secured a ninth straight win. In February 1867, Wednesday organised their inaugural fundraising concert at the Surrey Street Music Hall, which included the talents of Herr Schollhammer at the piano and Miss Goddard and Miss Twigg as vocalists. The cricketers also contributed with a rendition of the 'cricketer's song'. The opening game of 1867 included many men who would be pivotal in the early history of the football club, individuals such as Chambers, Anderson, Chatterton and Pashley. Wednesday were reminded of earlier times when eleven of the Wednesday club faced twenty of Owlerton in a Handicap Sweepstakes match at Hyde Park Cricket Ground. Wednesday had enjoyed its best decade since formation in terms of games played and membership numbers, and this led to an event that would ensure the name Wednesday would become known all over the world, but for their deeds in a totally different sport.

The Arrival of Football

A change to the working patterns of the 'populace' was arguably the main reason why association football grew at such a pace during the mid-nineteenth century. On the back of the Industrial Revolution, which brought huge social and religious reform, the 1847 and 1850 Factory Acts meant that employers could no longer decide the hours of work, and the workday was changed to correspond with the maximum number of hours that women and children could work. This quickly changed to apply to all employees as it became uneconomic to keep a factory open for just a male workforce. The overall leisure time for employees decreased, but life became more organised and punctual, with the opportunity for the pursuit of leisure activities more defined. The major change though, with regard to football, was the new rule that all work on a Saturday would end at 2.00 p.m., leaving the worker with a half day to spend at their leisure. As society adapted to these new working conditions, the game of football grew quickly and, inside a twenty-year period, the sport expanded from being a pastime played only in the public schools and universities to teams being formed in most of the cities, towns and villages of Britain. Men and boys now had time to play and watch this attractive new sport, which was fast, exciting and easy to play and follow. It was also highly competitive and involved passion, rivalry and loyalty based on families, neighbourhoods, workplaces, pubs and clubs. It is not difficult to see how the game quickly became a national pastime.

The medieval game of football had been played for several centuries, with games recorded in ancient China, Rome and Greece. In England, a form of 'mob' football saw whole towns and villages take part in a game that could take days to complete. An example of this is recorded in nearby Ashbourne way back in the mid-1660s, but the first real standardised rules originated from Cambridge University in the late 1840s. The game of football was actually recorded in Sheffield in 1831, 1844 and 1853, with the sport played on a regular basis in Penistone and Holmfirth. A version of the game was also recorded at Bent's Green in 1793 when six men of Norton, dressed in green, faced six men of Sheffield, dressed in red, in a three-day game. The town of Sheffield, of course, would play a crucial role in the early development of football as the formation of Sheffield FC in 1857 was accompanied by the emergence of what became known as the 'Sheffield Rules', which differed in various ways from those that came out of the public schools and universities. In those days, the sport was different to today's twenty-first-century product, with matches ranging from eleven to fifteen a side. Hacking, tripping and handling of the ball were all allowed, and even the shape of the ball was often more akin to the modern rugby ball. The actual game was also far removed from the modern game as the majority of the players tended to follow the ball around the field, not unlike the 'mob' football of old, with formations and tactics still several years away. Only the goalkeeper and two forwards were fairly static, with the latter spending all the match hanging around the opposition custodian. The penalty kick, throw in and crossbar were all still to feature in the rules as the sport evolved naturally as more and more of the working classes started to watch and take part in the pastime.

WEDNESDAY FOOTBALL CLUB OFFICIALS 1867–92

President

Benjamin Chatterton	1867-1868
Frank Chambers	1868-1870
Henry Hawksley	1870-1887
John Holmes	1887-

Secretary

John Marsh	1867-1874
William Littlehales	1874-1883
James Hoyland	1883-1885
J. B. Thompson	1885-1886
Jack Hudson (Joint)	1886-1888
George Cropper (Joint)	1886-1888
Harry Pearson	1888-1891
Arthur Dickinson	1891-

Vice Presidents

Frank Chambers	1867-1868
Henry Hawksley	1868 1870

William Littlehales	1869-1874 & 1885-1886
John Rodgers	1870-1872
Alfred Stacey	1872-1879
Charley Hill	1874-1880
Walter Fearnehough	1879-
John Holmes	1879-1887
William Heaton Stacey	1880-1887
Harry Ellis	1887-1891
Alfred Holmes	1887-
Charles H Vessey	1888-

The 1860s saw the game of association football played in the north of England under 'Sheffield rules', and in the south under 'Cambridge rules', which were revised and updated soon after the formation of the Football Association in 1863 – handling, tripping and hacking all being removed. By this time, Sheffield Club – formed by silver-plate manufacturer Nathaniel Creswick and wine merchant William Prest – had a new town rival in the shape of Hallam Football Club, with a 600-strong crowd attending the February 1861 meeting between the two. The sport was also spreading south with County and Forest soon to be formed in Nottingham. In 1861 the town of Sheffield could boast nine established clubs including the aforementioned Sheffield and Hallam plus Norton, Pitsmoor, York (a Broomhall Hotel), artillery engineer volunteers, Norfolk and Collegiate; numbers had risen to twenty-two within a year. It should be noted that in December 1862 Hallam faced Sheffield in the first football match played at Bramall Lane in a charitable game in aid of the Lancashire Distress Fund for cotton workers. With the town of Sheffield expanding at an increasing pace – population had reached 200,000 and was still climbing – there was a rising interest in health, fitness and sport, with football heavily promoted by Victorian society as a way of achieving all three objectives. The Sheffield FA was formed in March 1867, and it was against this backdrop that the members of Wednesday Club made the momentous decision to form a football section of the cricket club, mainly so members could be kept together during the winter months, although the rapid growth of the game was another factor. The meeting was held at the Adelphi Hotel on Wednesday 4 September 1867, with the proceedings duly reported in the local press.

SHEFFIELD WEDNESDAY CRICKET CLUB AND FOOTBALL CLUB

'At a general meeting held on Wednesday last, at the Adelphi Hotel, it was decided to form a football club in connection with the above influential cricket club, with the object of keeping together during the winter season the members of the cricket club. From the great unanimity which prevailed as to the desirability of forming the club, there is every reason to expect that it will take first rank. The office bearers were elected as follows: President, Mr. B. Chatterton; vice-president and treasurer, Mr. F. S. Chambers; hon. secretary, Mr. Jno. Marsh; assistant, Mr. Castleton; Committee: Messers Jno. Rodgers, Jno. Pashley, Wm. Pilch, Wm. Littlehales, Jno. White, C. Stokes, H. Bocking. Above sixty members were enrolled, without any canvas, some of them being the best players of the town'

Sheffield and Rotherham Independent, Friday 6 September 1867

With all the officials in place, and great interest in the venture from the members of the cricket club, Wednesday Football Club quickly secured a pitch in the Highfields district of the town near to where modern-day London Road and Abbeydale Road converge. It was once thought that Wednesday played where Highfields library is situated, but more recent research suggests the actual pitch was nearer to where the medical centre was subsequently built and where Highfield Place, Holland Road and Colver Road exist today. It was perhaps no coincidence that Wednesday chose that district of town as, back in the mid-nineteenth century, a private residence, Parkfield House, was a prominent feature in the area. This house was significant because in October 1857 the owner, solicitor Harry Waters Chambers, hosted a meeting there that led to the formation of Sheffield FC. The host also owned the lands around his residence, and it seems very likely that such a keen follower and player of the newly emerging sport would look kindly upon any request for permission to play on his land.

That first playing venue would simply have been a basic pitch and would certainly not have boasted any facilities to speak of. It should perhaps be noted though that a lack of 'home comforts' would not have significantly affected those early skirmishes as many players would dash straight from work, playing in their work clothes and boots, with one side just tying a handkerchief to their sleeves to distinguish themselves from the opposition. Players would occasionally hammer nails into their boots to aid balance on the poor quality pitches, and one can only imagine what sort of injuries that would have caused before the practise, thankfully, was superseded by the arrival of studded football boots in the latter part of the nineteenth century.

JOHN PASHLEY, 1ST COMMITTEE

John Pashley had the distinction of being the man that first proposed that a football club be formed from the cricket section. A brewery traveller – he worked for the Broomspring Lane Brewery Co. – Pashley was well known for playing both cricket and football, primarily for Wednesday and Pitsmoor. He also regularly competed in the various athletic days, and while secretary of Sheffield Norfolk FC he helped organise a joint sports day with Wednesday FC in 1872. Born in Doncaster in 1838, he was elected onto the first Wednesday FC committee, serving for just one season, but remained a keen supporter of the football club, travelling as a club official to a game at Spital in March 1877. Sadly, he died at the age of only forty-two at his Broomspring Lane home on 30 September 1881 after having fallen ill on the previous Saturday during a cricket match at Langwith. He was forced to stay overnight in the village and on his return home had seemingly recovered. However, he had a severe relapse and died from 'heart disease' soon after, leaving a widow but no children. His funeral was attended by Henry Hawksley, William Littlehales and William Fretwell, the Wednesday Club president, football and cricket club secretaries respectively.

No matter how basic the surroundings, it gave the football club its first real roots, and in mid-October the first game took place, with members playing an inter-club match. A week later on 19 October 1867, Wednesday visited Norfolk Park – the home of United Mechanics FC – and in their first 'proper' game scored three goals and four rouges to one recorded by their opponents. It should be explained at this point that the rouge was added to the 'Sheffield Rules' in 1861, borrowed from Eton College, when the goal was reduced from 8 yards wide to just 4 yards, with rouge flags then placed 4 yards either side. If the ball was 'put through' the main posts it was a goal, and if it was put through the outer markers and touched down, it was classed as a rouge. The concept was that if the game finished in a tie then rouges would decide the winner, but the rule was scrapped in 1868 – although modern-day Australian Rules Football has a similar scoring system.

The fledgling football section played the likes of Milton and Heeley before providing the first opposition for the newly formed Dronfield club – winning by 1 goal to 4 rouges in a field 'kindly lent by Mr S. Baggally Esq.'. In February 1868, what became known as the Cromwell Cup was offered for competition for any club under two years old. In the previous season, the first ever football trophy – donated by local theatre impresario Thomas Youdan, of the Alexandra Theatre and Opera House, and won by Hallam – was competed for in Sheffield. Wednesday, along with Garrick, Exchange and Wellington clubs, completed the entrants for the new tournament promoted by Oliver Cromwell – the manager of the Theatre Royal.

ALFRED WOOD

Born in Sheffield in 1846, Alf Wood played for Wednesday in their first season, appearing in the side that lifted the Cromwell Cup. The diminutive Wood, an optical brass turner, was described as a 'capital little forward' and was a member of the club from its formation. Like many of the members in those early years, he was a keen all-round sportsman, winning the 700-yard Handicap steeplechase at Wednesday's 1869 Athletics Day. Sadly, his story came to a premature end as after appearing for Wednesday against Fir Vale in March 1875, he took a trip to Scotland and subsequently caught a cold after leaving his travel blanket in another carriage. He never recovered, passing away in Sheffield at the tender age of twenty-nine on 6 April 1875. His friends started a subscription for donations for the benefit of his wife Emma and family; the Sheffield Association arranged a benefit match at Bramall Lane.

First Trophy

Wednesday kicked off the tournament on the first Saturday in February, on a day that saw Sheffield battered by fierce winds, sending chimney pots, slates and signs crashing to the ground. It was Wednesday who prevailed, comfortably beating Exchange by 4 goals and 3 rouges to 0 in a fourteen a-side game played at Myrtle Road – home of the MacKenzie Club. A week later, Garrick clinched their place in the Bramall Lane final and they were favourites to lift the trophy as their side contained seven of Hallam's best players. The stage was therefore set for the final and around 400 fans, the first paying spectators to watch Wednesday, witnessed a hard-fought game. Garrick played with the wind in the first period and was unlucky early on, when the Wednesday 'keeper missed his kick and the ball, bizarrely described as the 'Giant Shang' in contemporary reports, rebounded from the foot of the goalpost. The Wednesday side, containing Denton, Whelan, Charles Stokes, Jenkinson, Broomhead and Alf Wood, had the conditions in their favour in the second half, but at the close neither side had scored. It was then agreed by both teams to play on, with the first side to score winning the trophy. Wednesday won the toss and again had the wind in their favour, and with Captain John Marsh in fine form, they duly scrambled home the 'golden' goal 10 minutes into the additional time, much to the delight of their partisan following. Captain Marsh was presented with the cup by Cromwell, who was enjoying his benefit year, on stage at the Theatre Royal on the evening of Monday 16 March 1868. Wednesday FC could look back on their maiden season with great pride, a trophy secured, and the new boys firmly established on the burgeoning Sheffield football scene. It should also be noted that membership was such in that inaugural campaign that the club also ran a second team, with the first recorded result being a match at Garrick reserves, which was lost by a rouge.

WILLIAM BROMLEY CASTLETON, 1ST ASSISTANT SECRETARY

Engraver William Castleton was only in his mid-twenties (born in June 1843) when he was appointed to the role of assistant secretary on the club's formation. He aided club secretary Marsh for two seasons before relinquishing the position in 1869. William, who married Frances in 1873 and had a son, Harold, was living with his parents at No. 26 Gloucester Street when he was part of that pivotal day in September 1867. In December 1872, William was involved in an unsavoury incident in Sheffield when he was mugged, along with an acquaintance, as they walked home from Midland Station. The pair were badly beaten and later found by two policemen, who took them home in a cab. Castleton became a prominent cricket umpire in later life, but was forced to retire in 1902 due to failing eyesight. However, a year of treatment saw William return to the cricket square, although he sadly died five years later in June 1908 aged sixty-four.

To complete a successful campaign, Sheffield Wednesday Football and Cricket Club held their first ever 'Athletic Sports Day' on 30 March 1868, with members and friends providing some generous and numerous prizes for the event at the Bramall Lane Cricket Ground. The day started at just past 1.00 p.m. with the 120-yard dash, and the event was hailed a great success with committeeman John White organising all the various races while also competing. He finished third in the 'putting the stone' – an old Scottish discipline similar to the modern-day shot-put. Other events included the 300-yard steeplechase, 1-mile walk (won by Alf Wood), 120-yard maiden race (won by committee man Fry) and even a sack race. A healthy crowd of around 2,000 enjoyed the inaugural event and ensured the club's initial impact on the Sheffield sporting scene was absolute.

JOHN MARSH, 1ST SECRETARY

Johnny Marsh was arguably the most important individual of the club's fledgling years, being Wednesday's team first captain and honorary secretary. Born around 1843 in Thurlstone – a small village near Sheffield – Marsh was living with his parents at nearby Dunford Bridge in 1851 and later in the decade moved to Sheffield to begin an apprenticeship as an engraver at John Rodgers & Sons. He subsequently became great friends with John Rodgers Jnr and the pair became enthusiastic competitors at cricket and football as well as being noted as fine singers. Marsh is first recorded playing for Wednesday CC in the early 1860s and served on the committee between the years of 1864 and 1868. He was also assistant secretary for a time and served as cricket club secretary for three years (1869–72), but it is his link with the football club for which he is best known.

It is believed that Marsh played in all of the club's early games and certainly was in the side that lifted Wednesday's first trophy – the Cromwell Cup. He was a universally popular figure in sporting circles, being a no-nonsense defender – in the aforementioned cup win he was noted as 'putting his toe in with precision, celerity and force for which he is so well known'. It was also said that occasionally 'brandy was called to resuscitate the prostrate foe', and there is no doubt that Marsh led by example and was Wednesday's first outstanding captain. He remained a mainstay of the side for seven seasons, as well as captaining the Sheffield FA in their first ever inter-association games with London in the early 1870s. He returned to his native Thurlstone in 1874 and became the landlord of the Crystal Palace public house in the village as well as continuing to work as an engraver. He duly formed a new football team connected to the public house, but it was while playing for that side that he fell awkwardly and suffered a badly broken arm. The fracture never healed correctly – Marsh even travelled to London in an attempt to have the break reset, although the procedure was never undertaken. Sadly, he slipped into depression due to the pain from his arm, which was bound in steel bands, and a general slump in the local iron trade. He would never recover and passed away aged thirty-seven to consumption in Thurlstone on 21 April 1880, leaving a widow and four children. It was a sad end for a man who played such a pivotal role in the early years of today's multi-million pound football club.

The close season of 1868/69 saw several of the early founder members give way to new blood when the club held its first annual general meeting at the Adelphi, now run by Ralph Armfield (who joined the committee). Departures included President Chatterton (replaced by Frank Chambers) and committee men Bocking and Stokes. The local press, rather surprisingly, failed to report on the club's fortunes. All that is known is that several games were arranged against local sides Broomhall, Heeley, MacKenzie, Dronfield, United Mechanics, Pitsmoor and Wellington, but sadly no record has survived of any actual results. It was, however, recorded that the club's second annual sports day, held at Bramall Lane, was another success, with the boys of the Sheffield Charity School invited to the proceedings – a sign of the club's standing was that the Lord Mayor and Wednesday supporter Thomas Moore presented the prizes. Around 2,000 people attended the event, although it was stated that receipts only just covered expenses. Pilch, George Sampson, Littlehales and Rodgers all featured in a busy programme of events, with the highlight being the quarter mile race that boasted twenty-nine competitors. After the final event, the youngsters ran a handicap race and after several wagers had been placed on the result, all the silver and copper was shared out among the boys. They were also given refreshments by the onsite caterers, Messers Bland and Robinson, with biscuits, ale and ginger beer all on the menu. The youngsters duly left the ground to great applause after singing the national anthem, accompanied by the band of the Hallamshire Rifles, who Wednesday had engaged for the day.

FRANCIS SMITH CHAMBERS, 1ST VICE PRESIDENT

Frank Chambers was born in Sheffield in October 1836 and would remain a keen sportsman throughout his adult life. Frank, who never married, was the football club's first ever vice president, serving one season before replacing Ben Chatterton as president in 1868. He held the office for two years before reverting back to a committee role in 1870. Frank held a variety of roles during his working life, which included cotton spinner, hardware merchant (as his father Charles had been), brewery manager and then simply a brewer. He also spent three seasons as president of Wednesday CC (1867–70) and was a regular helper at the annual club athletics days. He passed away, aged fifty-five, on 5 April 1892, just eighteen months after his father joined the 'great majority'.

Thankfully, that media 'blip' with regard to football activities proved temporary, and Wednesday kicked off the next season with a visit to Pitsmoor before the 'Heeleyites' won 3-1 at Meersbrook Park. The name of Clegg was mentioned for the first time in a Wednesday team, although it's not recorded if it was William or Charles. Two weeks later, both of the Clegg brothers appeared in the defeat to Broomhall at Highfields – a week after Wednesday had beaten the same opponents at the same venue – but on this occasion they appeared for the opposition. This provided an early example of a change of allegiance, which was commonplace throughout the 1860s and 1870s. In an era that was almost totally amateur, players could play for as many clubs as they wanted and would often chase glory – the defection of several Hallam players to Garrick in the aforementioned Cromwell Cup being a prime example – until rules were introduced and players became 'cup tied'. It was an indication of how football was still in its infancy by the fact that Wednesday played eighteen first team games in their third season, but faced only five different opponents: Broomhall were met on five occasions; United Mechanics four; Pitsmoor three; and Heeley, Fir Vale and Dronfield twice.

BENJAMIN CHATTERTON, 1ST PRESIDENT

Despite only being involved with the football club for one season, Ben Chatterton (b. 1803) held a vital place in the club's early history as a founding member and first president. Before the formation of the football team, Chatterton was a well-known cricketer, first joining Wednesday around 1845 and the committee in 1852. He appeared in the first game played at Bramall Lane and played for Wednesday as well as Sheffield CC in many of the high profile games of the era. He was presented with a silver cup by Wednesday in 1863 in recognition of being the club's best bowler. He served as Cricket Club president for four years during the 1860s, and returned to the club's committee in 1868 after having led the football club through its inaugural season. Away from sport, Chatterton was a man of considerable means – a prominent financial agent – and was noted in 1881 as living off income from property with his five children, wife and two domestic servants in the more salubrious part of town. He served with distinction on the Sheffield town council between 1868 and 1880, being re-elected three times by the citizens of the rapidly expanding town. He lived to the age of seventy-two before passing away at his Nether Edge home on 16 October 1902, leaving a legacy in both sporting and public life.

The club's third annual athletics day also took place and it was noted that 'amongst many enterprising clubs none have hitherto displayed greater energy and tact than the Wednesday in promoting the healthful outdoor recreations and amusement'. Around 3,000 people attended the event, with Wednesday showing a profit on the day's activities after spending £75 to secure the ground and hire the Chesterfield Prize Band. Club officials White, Chambers and Hawksley took the roles of starter, judge and clerk of the course respectively. The 120-yard flat race saw Charles Clegg take the honours while another Wednesday footballer, George Sampson, was victorious in the 300-yard handicap steeplechase from William Clegg in second. The day also saw a theatrical race run with all seven competitors engaged at the Theatre Royal. All the runners wore theatrical costumes, borrowed from the theatre, and caused much merriment when they lined up for the start. Victory went to the Native Red Indian (Mr Sievewright) with a sailor (Mr Cleveland) finishing second. It was also significant that the various events had taken place, for the first time, on the popular day of Easter Monday – a sign of how quickly Wednesday had risen in popularity, driven on by enthusiastic officials, in a relatively short space of time.

HENRY BOCKING, 1ST COMMITTEE

Like all the individuals who were founders of the football section, Henry Bocking was primarily a keen member of Wednesday Cricket Club, first playing in the early 1860s. Sheffield-born in 1840, Henry played the vast majority of his club cricket with Wednesday, although in October 1862 he could be found playing for Hallam CC in a unique three a-side £50 single-wicket match at Hyde Park. A table knife grinder, Henry joined the football club's first committee, but served only one season before relinquishing the position to concentrate on Wednesday's summer activities. He won the 'best batter' award at Wednesday in 1864 and continued to play until the late 1870s – also serving on the committee between 1877 and 1882. He was father to eight children, and in September 1887 was one of fifty-seven passengers injured in a rail disaster at Doncaster, which left twenty-five dead. Henry had attended two days racing at Doncaster and was returning for a third day when disaster struck as his train, waiting at Hexthorpe, was run into by the Liverpool–Hull train instantly killing twenty-three people in the Sheffield carriages. Thankfully, Henry survived, suffering a broken leg, and after a spell in Doncaster Royal Infirmary he returned home. He lived until May 1906 before passing away in Sheffield, aged sixty-six.

Ground Change

The 1870/71 season saw Wednesday change homes as they moved from Highfields to take up residence at Myrtle Road, which was situated just off the newly built Queens Road in Heeley. Contemporary reports suggest the pitch was situated between Myrtle Road and Midhill Road and was sloped towards an old quarry overlooking Olive Grove – the current site of the Sheffield council works department and more importantly, an eventual home for Wednesday. The new ground would be rented from Mr Bailey of Bank Farm, Heeley, with Wednesday paying a total of £8 and 3s for the use of the pitch from 1st October until 1 March, which included labour costs for erecting the goal posts. The date of the club's first home game at their new venue cannot be pinpointed exactly as Wednesday opened the new season with first and second team fixtures, in October 1870, against MacKenzie Club. Unfortunately for historians, their opponents also played their home fixtures at the exact same ground. It seems likely that the first team game against MacKenzie was in fact Wednesday's first Myrtle Road home fixture, although the report of the game suggests otherwise. The club's AGM had resulted in John Rodgers being elected as vice president, replacing Hawksley who moved up to president, while the aforementioned opening fixture against MacKenzie Club saw Wednesday actually kick-off the game, despite having a two player numerical disadvantage. The missing men did eventually put in an appearance. The match was significant for being the first game for which a team is named in full in the press report, recorded below for posterity:

J. Marsh, C, Mills, W. E. Clegg, J. C. Clegg, J. Hollingsworth, G. H. Sampson, F. Butler, T. Cawthron, W. Ward, C. Stokes, H. Parker, J. Anthony and G. Anthony.

Included in the side was captain Marsh plus committeeman John Hollingsworth and George Sampson, while 'little' Frank Butler and 'Barnsley Tom' Cawthron also appeared in a game where Sampson (son of Henry) scored the only goal for Wednesday. Incidentally, the game was also the first reported instance of an umpire in a Wednesday fixture – eventually each side would have their own umpire on the field of play. The win was the first of six consecutive victories that stretched into the New Year, with Wednesday also failing to concede a goal. A single goal win against Broomhall at Eccleshall Road, in a game reduced to 60 minutes due to a 'heavy pitch', followed, with John Edward Deans scoring the game's only goal. Wednesday then won against Dean's old side, Heeley, in a fourteen a-side challenge match at Meersbrook Park.

WILLIAM HENRY FRY, 1ST COMMITTEE

Sheffield born in 1841, William Fry was a silver engraver and member of Wednesday Cricket Club, having joined the committee in 1866. He was subsequently on the first committee when the football section was formed. Like many of his peers he was a great lover of all sports, and at Wednesday's athletics day in 1868 he won the 120-yard 'maiden race' for first time competitors. He remained on the committee of the football club for the first two seasons of their history and remained closely connected to the cricket club for the remainder of his life, regularly attending meetings throughout the 1860s and 1870s, having been appointed assistant secretary in 1868. Sadly he passed away, aged only forty-three, at his Highfield Place residence on 28 February 1885. His wife Hannah outlived her husband by an astonishing fifty-two years.

The Queens Hotel grounds then hosted what was described as the 'first great football match of the season in Sheffield' when a combined Derbyshire side challenged Wednesday – a club that was now commonly considered one of the best in Sheffield. The game proved one-sided as Wednesday raced to a 7-0 win before both sets of players and officials retired to the Adelphi to dine and enjoy 'songs, glee and recitations'. The return fixture, in early January 1871 at Osmaston Park, was played under 'Sheffield Rules', although the sides agreed that touching or catching of the ball was not allowed. Another handsome win for Wednesday followed, with new president Henry Hawksley in the side. The

WILLIAM LITTLEHALES, 1ST COMMITTEE

Of the men who founded the football section of Wednesday, William Littlehales was one of only two not from Yorkshire; he was born in Birmingham on 2 June 1834. He followed in the footsteps of his father by becoming a gold and silver engraver, which prompted a move to Sheffield in the 1870s. After moving north he became a prominent member of the MacKenzie club, appearing for them on the football field. He suffered a terrible blow in July 1867 when his wife of nine years, Sarah Anne, passed away. Whether it was coincidental or not, William then threw himself into his sporting pleasures – he never remarried – and was duly elected onto the first Wednesday FC committee. He was an enthusiastic playing member of both sports and was a regular goalscorer for the football section in the late 1860s/early 1870s. He served on the committee for two seasons and then as vice president until 1874 when he replaced Marsh as secretary. He served with distinction for nine years as well as becoming a chief figure on the committee of the Sheffield FA. A father to two boys – looked after by his mother after the loss of his wife – Littlehales was an astute and popular figure in Sheffield sporting circles. It was only failing health that caused his resignation from the position of Wednesday FC secretary in 1883, although he continued his association by becoming treasurer for two seasons and then vice president for a single season. He was still an active member of Wednesday FC while also running the Midland Hotel on Cross Turner Street. He died on Sunday 24 January 1886, aged fifty-one, after contributing a key role in the development of both facets of the Wednesday club.

away party did not arrive back in Sheffield until 2.00 a.m. the following morning after the post-match celebrations – the early days of association football often seemed more of a social occasion than a sporting one!

The early part of the season indicated an increasing membership as third team fixtures were introduced. Wednesday beat Sheffield-based Oxford Club 3-0 in October 1870. First team games followed, in the New Year, at Myrtle Road against MacKenzie, Heeley and Broomhall (the club's only recorded defeat in a successful campaign) before the curtain came down on the season, on the last Saturday in February, when Fir Vale were beaten 3-0 at Wednesday's new ground – player of the season George Sampson was described by the local scribe as a 'veritable giant'. It was recorded that Wednesday played a total of twenty-five games in that season at all levels, recording fifteen wins and seven draws. A few weeks later, Easter Monday saw the club hold their sports day at Bramall Lane, with fifteen races and several qualifying heats. To entertain the crowd, Wednesday engaged the services of the Yeomanry Cavalry Band. Player Sampson was again to the fore, winning the 300-yard steeplechase for the third year running.

JOHN W. WHITE, 1ST COMMITTEE

Born in Sheffield in 1842, John White was elected to the football club's first committee after having played, and also served on the cricket club's committee between 1864 and 1866 – he was also vice president for one season (1870). His association with the football club lasted two seasons, and although there is no record of him actually playing football he did assist at the club's athletic sports days. After serving as an apprentice he took over his father's business, and in 1871 was trading as a builder and valuer from his Hartshead home, employing twelve men in his business. He also served for many years on the town council, being noted in both 1869 and 1878, but his later life proved somewhat of a mystery and it's believed he died at a young age in Sheffield late in 1880, leaving his wife Jane and several children.

The movement that commenced in the late 1860s to increase the provision of public parks and the 1871 Bank Holiday Act both served to increase space and the opportunity for exercise, and clubs continued to be formed around the Sheffield area. The Wednesday AGM, held in September 1871, saw the members vote to keep catching in their rule book. The new season opened with a Cawthron double helping Wednesday to win a fourteen a-side game at Attercliffe Christ Church 3-0 – an opening fixture that became the traditional curtain raiser, except for a solitary season when bad weather intervened, until 1883. The game against Mackenzie at Myrtle Road, classed as an away match, saw Wednesday start well, but unfortunately after around 20 minutes the ball suddenly burst and the game was abandoned after no one was able to obtain a replacement. A few weeks later, Wednesday faced Rotherham for the first time, winning 4-1 at the Clifton Lane Cricket Ground, while a week later Derby St Andrews visited Myrtle Road and were soundly beaten 8-0, with Reaney grabbing a treble. The side on that day included popular captain Marsh, Charles and William Clegg, Walter Fearnehough and Frank Butler. Both sides duly retired to the Adelphi for the accustomed post-game festivities.

WILLIAM FREDERICK PILCH, 1ST COMMITTEE

Although born in Norwich in 1840, William Pilch spent most of his life in Sheffield, becoming a popular member of the town's sporting scene. He was the nephew of the famous cricketer Fuller Pilch – the man who took

Marsden's single-wicket crown in 1828 – and became the first man to open a sports outfitter's shop in Sheffield, based near to the Adelphi Hotel, which was 'the only complete cricket and lawn tennis outfitter in Sheffield'. He was in his physical prime in the 1860s and 1870s, participating in all the sports that appealed to the 'gentry' of the town, such as cricket, football, fencing, gymnastics and skating. As well as being on the football club's first committee for a single season, William also served on the cricket club's committee for the same period of time in addition to being the founder of the Sheffield Fencing and Skating Clubs and treasurer of the town's gymnasium club. A multi-talented sportsman, William also won several medals as an amateur boxer and played football and cricket for Wednesday, only retiring from the former after suffering a dislocated knee. He married Matlock girl Alice, and after his playing career ended William continued to run his sports shop – it was said he never missed a Yorkshire CCC game at Bramall Lane. Despite only serving on the football committee for one season, Pilch often lent a hand when required, stewarding at the club's 1878 athletics day. He later became president of the Rustlings Lawn Tennis Club and was still vice president when he suffered a seizure on Christmas Eve 1927, dying the following day at his Broomhall home, leaving a son, who was named Fuller after his famous relative. He reached the grand old age of eighty-seven and was, by many years, the last surviving member of the gentlemen who formed Wednesday FC.

The highlight of the football calendar in Sheffield came in early December 1871 when, at Bramall Lane, the first representative game took place as Sheffield FA beat the London FA 3-1 – under Sheffield rules – with the strength of Wednesday shown by the fact that seven of the home side were drawn from the club's ranks – namely Marsh, Sampson, Wood, William Carr, Hollingsworth and the Clegg siblings. Before the return game was played with Derby in mid-January, Wednesday found themselves in uncharted waters as they lost two consecutive games for the first time in their history, with a subsequent defeat to Broomhall stretching the barren run to three games – somewhat of a mini crisis such was the club's overall results up until that point. The visit to Derbyshire saw Wednesday face Derby St Andrews with a rather random kick-off time of 2.40 p.m. The outcome was another comprehensive victory as goals from Marsh, Tom Butler, Hollingsworth and club vice president Littlehales wrapped up a 4-0 win in a game where a charge by Walter Fearnehough, on the opposition custodian, was commented upon as being 'extremely judged and timed'. The teams then retired to Mr Sims' Clarendon Hotel to toast success and drown sorrows in equal measure.

CHARLES STOKES, 1ST COMMITTEE

Charles Stokes holds a unique place in the history of Sheffield football as he was not only a founder member of Wednesday FC but is also considered to have founded Sheffield United. Born in Sheffield on 30 December 1847, Charles' father was a silversmith and electroplate manufacturer, and it was due to a relatively affluent background that his son could train to become a dentist. He duly qualified and became an eminent man in his profession, trading from his London Road practice as well as being chairman of the dental board at the Royal Hospital. Stokes was also a keen sportsman, running and football being among his main passions – his training routine included regular runs from his Highfields home to Bamford. He joined the Heeley club in 1864, and after winning a first prize in their 1865 sports day would take part in athletics days, not just in Sheffield, over the next four years, which brought forth another fifty-five wins and sixteen seconds from seventy-six races. He also played cricket, joining the Wednesday Cricket Club in 1866, and it was this link that directly led to Stokes being named on that first ever Wednesday FC committee. Stokes was a player and committeeman at Wednesday and played in the side that lifted the Cromwell Cup – he was not noted as being a brilliant footballer but was quick and committed. Before joining Wednesday he'd appeared for Milton and Broomhall, while in the early 1870s was appearing in the colours of Brincliffe alongside George Sampson. During his early life he was also a reputed amateur violinist, helping organise the Sheffield Music Festival, and was said to possess a gentle hand and strong pull – two ideal traits for a dentist! A father of seven children – three of whom died before reaching five – Stokes is perhaps better known for his founding role of Wednesday's cross city rivals. This commenced in 1869 when he joined the body that managed Bramall Lane before joining the ground committee in 1875. It was the successful staging of a FA Cup semi-final at Bramall Lane in 1889 that directly led to Stokes' proposing the formation of a football club. He served as chairman from formation until his death in 1913 – the year in which his son, Percy, joined the Blades' board. In addition he served for many years as committeeman and treasurer to Yorkshire CCC, was the first treasurer when the Sheffield and Hallamshire FA was formed in 1887 and maintained a link with Wednesday Cricket Club, serving as vice president in the early 1890s. Stokes, who was said to be a 'typical Sheffielder' immensely proud of his birthplace, passed away at his home aged sixty-six on 8 October 1913, having left a lasting sporting legacy to the city.

A week later, MacKenzie won the toss and 'kicked down the hill' at Myrtle Road, but a late header from Frank Butler meant Wednesday gained the spoils. The next fixture proved controversial as Wednesday fans were sure the ball had gone out of play in the build up to the only goal and were somewhat perplexed when the Heeley players appealed to the umpire, who promptly gave the goal. It is perhaps comforting to the modern-day supporter that match officials have been the cause of controversy from the very early days.

A comfortable 3-0 home win followed in the return game with Attercliffe before the season was concluded, on the last Saturday of February, with a Myrtle Road clash against Fir Vale. Unfortunately, the weather on that final day was reported as being 'about as bad as it could be for football' and several games across Sheffield were postponed, with two players not arriving at Myrtle Road as they did not expect the match to go ahead. Various other absentees meant Wednesday could only muster eight men to Fir Vale's ten, although the home side's numbers did increase with the half-time arrival of Wood. Unsurprisingly, Wednesday struggled against superior numbers, but battled gamely before losing 1-0 in a low key end to the season. Wednesday won twelve and lost eleven of the twenty-four games played in the season. It should also be noted that the 1871/72 campaign was significant as the practice of allowing alcoholic refreshment to the players after a match was discontinued. Before such time, the winners shared out a gallon of beer while the losers had to drown their sorrows with half as much. The club's fifth athletics sports day took place at Bramall Lane in April 1872 when, for the first and only time, the event was jointly hosted along with fellow Sheffield side Norfolk Football Club – Wednesday renewing ties with former committeeman Pashley, who was Norfolk's secretary. Unfortunately for all concerned, the weather was unseasonably cold and a heavy fall of snow blanketed Sheffield the day before meaning conditions were treacherous underfoot. The poor weather also badly affected the attendance, with less than half the usual crowd, many of those being driven away, when the proceedings were hit by a heavy hail storm.

However, the event was completed to a satisfactory conclusion – even a race where the competitors where paired in couples and blindfolded – to bring the curtain down on another progressive season for the fledgling club. Before the new campaign commenced, Wednesday welcomed Walter Mills onto the club's committee, while Alfred Stacey and Rodgers swapped roles behind the scenes with the former becoming vice president and latter returning to the committee. The first action of the new season took place on the first Saturday of October 1872, with Wednesday winning 4-2 at Attercliffe with popular attacker Cawthron among the goalscorers against the 'Christians'. The positive start continued with a 2-0 win at Heeley before Wednesday drew against Broomhall at Ecclesall Road with Sampson 'putting through' for Wednesday. A week later, Wednesday were well represented as the Sheffield FA beat their London counterparts 4-0 at Bramall Lane before Wednesday lost 1-0 in a fourteen a-side challenge match against the Derbyshire Association at the same venue – the first 'home' game played by Wednesday at the Bramall Lane Cricket Ground. Until 1887, the vast majority of the club's high-profile home fixtures would be moved to the venue, mainly because it was possible to charge for admission and was regarded as the best sporting ground in the town. Around 500 fans watched Wednesday face the 'peak county' and the defeat was mainly attributed to the fact that Wednesday played their football in a rather more 'scientific' way than their opponents with 'Little Frank' Butler sent 'spinning head over heels' by opponent Gadsby during the contest.

JOHN RODGERS, 1ST COMMITTEE

Like his great friend Johnny Marsh, Sheffield-born John Rodgers passed away at a tragically young age, being taken in his sleep on 22 December 1876 aged thirty-six after contracting consumption. The pair had first become friends when Marsh started his apprenticeship with John's father, and both were keen sportsmen, playing cricket and then the new sport of football. John served for one summer on the cricket club's committee – he was a prominent fast bowler and a year later was on the first committee of the new football section. He served Wednesday FC for three seasons (1867–70) in that role before becoming vice president for two more years (1870–72). He rejoined the cricket club committee in 1870 and stepped back onto the football committee in 1872, serving on both bodies until his much lamented death. An engraver and lithographer, serving his apprenticeship in his father's business, John also reported on both cricket and football for the *Sheffield and Rotherham Independent*, and such was his popularity that, despite poor weather on the day of his funeral, numerous of his football and cricket friends assembled to pay their respects. He left a widow and two sons.

A single goal win at Fir Vale followed with the name of William Heaton Stacey then appearing among the Wednesday goalscorers for the first time, grabbing the winner in a victory at Brincliffe. It would not be until the second Saturday of January that Wednesday actually played their first game of the season at Myrtle Road with a third consecutive 1-0 victory – this time over old adversaries Heeley – continuing another successful season. The return fixture against Broomhall was then won at Myrtle Road – Bob Gregory making his first appearance for the club – prior to Wednesday going 'out of county' for the return match against the Derbyshire FA. The game was played under quite awful conditions in Chesterfield, on a snowbound frozen pitch with a bitter northern wind blowing throughout the game - those football pioneers were hardy folk and one wonders what possible combination of weather conditions were actually needed for a game to be postponed!

WILLIAM MOSFORTH

There is no doubt that Billy Mosforth was one of the greatest players that Sheffield has ever produced, aged only nineteen when he won the first of nine England caps. In an era when individualism was king, Billy was unchallenged as the most exciting player of his generation. He first appeared for Wednesday in 1875 and rapidly rose to win a national call up, when the England side was dominated by ex-Public school and university players. Billy was a fast, clever left winger, and an all-round athlete, competing for many years in various club's sports days. Although initially called the 'pocket Hercules' he became known as the 'little wonder' and this nickname stuck for the remainder of his career as Billy's mazy wing play lit up football matches in Sheffield. He was a huge favourite with the Sheffield sporting public, as well as achieving unprecedented fame nationally, and although small in stature – he stood 5ft 3ins – Mosforth became known for his incredible dribbling skills and clinical finishing. Born in Sheffield, on 2 January 1858, he was described as 'one of the most determined little forwards in England' and was a member of the Wednesday committee for five years, from 1880, while also playing cricket for Hallam, being a noted fast bowler. He forged a great left wing partnership with Herbert Newbould and won a plethora of medals in Wednesday colours, whilst also appearing in the club's first FA Cup tie. In 1882 he appeared in two FA Cup semi-finals and two England matches, inside a period of only ten days, while it was his dialogue with John Holmes that finally resulted in professionalism being adopted. The indomitable and plucky Mosforth enjoyed a benefit game in 1888, and had totalled six goals in 25 FA Cup games when a knee injury ended his career, after having appeared in Sheffield United's first fixture. After retiring, he was a licensee for the remainder of his working life and passed away on 11 July 1929 in Fir Vale (Northern General) Hospital, cremated at Crookes cemetery four days later.

After the shock defeat earlier in the season, Wednesday gained their revenge thanks to a 2-1 win with William Clegg scoring the late winner with his shot 'just passing underneath the tape'. It should be noted that the solid crossbar did not enter the FA rule book until 1882 – after being introduced in Sheffield – with rope and then tape used to signify the desired height prior to that date.

In fact, in the early years of organised football the ball only needed to pass between the goal posts at any height whatsoever, although as the sport grew this did lead to many a disagreement over whether a goal had been scored. It was not until 1876 that the standardised FA rules included the need for a tape to signify the height of the goal. The town of Sheffield was hugely influential in shaping the rules of the modern-day game, introducing the goalkeeper, neutral referee, corner kick, corner flag, throw-in, goal kick, indirect free kick, half-time, cup ties, trophies, the concept of players being 'cup tied', extra time and even heading of the ball. Another idea pioneered in Sheffield was the concept of playing matches for the benefit of various charitable causes, with Wednesday providing the majority of the players when a Town versus County match was played on Shrove Tuesday 1873, in aid of the Cherry Tree Orphanage. The 1872/73 campaign ended with a quartet of Myrtle Road fixtures, commencing with a 5-0 win for the first team over Fir Vale.

A surprise 4-0 defeat to Attercliffe was a shock for the senior side before club spirits were lifted after a mixed team beat Rotherham 9-0. The season would end on a positive note on the first Saturday in March when a brace apiece from William Orton and Bailey secured a 4-0 win against Brincliffe. Before attention could switch to the summer game of cricket, the club still had to organise their sixth annual athletics day; club officials were again successful in securing Easter Monday. Their hard work was rewarded with a splendid crowd of around 4,000 – a figure which was in excess of any that had so far been recorded for a football game in Sheffield. Unfortunately, the number of competitors was somewhat meagre compared to previous years, although all races went ahead as scheduled. The winners included Arliss West, in the 120-yard flat race, and the novelty race saw competitors tied in pairs, blindfolded and required to turn a somersault every time the starter pistol was fired by club president Hawksley. The club's AGM of September 1873 saw the name of Walter Fearnehough appear on the list of committeemen for the first time. William Stacey also joined the working committee while continuing to play for the club's first eleven. Wednesday also reported a cash balance of £38 – a handsome sum in those days – a not inconsiderable surplus for a purely amateur club who had only been in existence for six years and whose main income stream was from members' subscriptions.

CHARLES HILL

Charley Hill was a Wednesday man through and through, remarking at the club's 1878 sports day dinner that he 'was born, christened and married on a Wednesday'. Born in the town around 1810, he was widely regarded as the life and soul of most social gatherings with his droll and outlandish speeches making him popular at sporting get togethers. He was primarily involved with Wednesday Cricket Club and served from 1862–1880, initially on the committee before becoming vice president in 1874 – he was also football club vice president during the same time frame. He first joined the football committee in 1871, often helping out on athletic days, but sadly became afflicted with 'softening of the brain' and never recovered, passing away on 1 June 1882.

The new season opened with a twelve a-side encounter at Attercliffe, won 4-0 with the Clegg brothers, Frank Butler and Cawthron all scoring. The first senior game of the season at Myrtle Road, versus Broomhall, saw comments that the grass was too long and badly affected any 'scientific exhibition of play'. A fortnight later a treble from Hathersley helped Wednesday to a 5-0 victory against Exchange Brewery. Home games against Fir Vale and Heeley followed before captain Marsh found he was forced to start a twelve a-side game at Rotherham with only eight players after several of his side failed to appear – the understrength Wednesday side narrowly losing 1-0. This season also saw Wednesday play over the Christmas period, with a visiting Derbyshire side routed 6-0 with early club legends Charles Clegg, Frank Butler, Gregory and Anthony all 'putting through' for Wednesday.

The return game with Rotherham ended in a comfortable 2-0 win. The early February 1874 victory at Fir Vale – played on hilly ground at Shirecliffe Lane – was significant as William Stacey was handed the captaincy, it's believed for the first time, while an outstanding performance from Gregory helped the away side to victory. The last reported game of the season took place at the Derwent Rowing Club in Derby where an entertaining game ensued against Derbyshire, watched by an enthusiastic crowd of 2,000, although neither side could beat the respective goalkeepers. Although brought forward from the usual Easter Monday date, the club's athletics day continued to thrive with the 1874 instalment including a bicycle race. The Wednesday sports day though had not only earned a reputation for excellence among the good folk of Sheffield, but also among the entrants from such diverse locations as London, Liverpool, Manchester, Derby, Halifax and Nottingham. Prior to the start of the following season, another link with the individuals that formed the football section was broken as Marsh announced at the club's AGM that he was stepping down from his role as club secretary and playing captain. He was roundly thanked for his services by all in attendance, with vice president Littlehales replacing Marsh in the administrative role and William Stacey taking over as playing captain – his brother Fred also joined the committee. The 1874/75 campaign began with a win at Attercliffe (Cawthron with the only goal) before a gap in the early fixture list meant the club members held an inter-club practice game.

A week later, Wednesday experienced a disastrous afternoon at the Pitsmoor Cricket Grounds when they could only field nine men and crashed 4-0 to Fir Vale. This was all forgotten a week later when Wednesday met up again with former captain Marsh, providing the first opponents for his Thurlstone Crystal Palace team. There was great interest in the game, and around thirty players and friends of Marsh travelled from Victoria station by special carriage to nearby Penistone before being directed to a 'capital field' just outside Thurlstone. A bumper crowd of around 500 watched the challenge match – won 4-0 by Wednesday – before all concerned adjourned to the public house for a 'meat tea' and post-match drinks. A win at old rivals Heeley followed a week later before several Wednesday men were again called up by the Sheffield FA to face the London FA. It would be another month before the club's first team played again, with Wednesday's second team beating the first fourteen of Exchange Brewery at Myrtle Road before home and away second and third team games against Norfolk Park. The opening Saturday of December 1874 saw Wednesday welcome Her Majesty's 105th Regiment to Myrtle Road, winning 1-0 thanks to a strike from William Wardley. The result of a scheduled game against Broomhall was unfortunately not recorded in the local press, although it was noted that a five-goal individual haul from William Orton helped the reserves triumph 8-0 at Norfolk Park.

THOMAS JOSEPH ANDERSON

Thomas Anderson was born into a cricketing family along with his brother George, becoming a prominent player with Yorkshire CCC. Born in Aiskew, North Yorkshire, in May 1831, Thomas moved to Sheffield to take up a position as clerk in the estate offices of the Duke of Norfolk. However, his first love was sports and he eventually drifted into the position of football and cricket reporter for the *Sheffield Daily Telegraph*. Described as 'kind-hearted, genial and a generous man with a large circle of friends', Thomas was a real mainstay of Wednesday Cricket and football club in the 1860s and 1870s, being first recorded as cricket vice president in 1862. He actually spent the following year in America, but returned to serve as cricket secretary between 1863 and 1869, and then again between 1874 and 1875. In October 1867 he was presented with a tea and coffee service in recognition of his efforts during the past five years, and as a token of high esteem and respect in which he was held by fellow cricketers. His link to the football section was relatively brief, having only served on the committee for two years from 1868. His first love certainly was the summer game, and he also acted as official scorer for Wednesday CC. He reported on sporting matters for twenty years. He also worked as a tillage agent (an individual who prepares land for the cultivation of crops), but suffered a long illness after being seized with paralysis while reporting a cricket game at Bramall Lane. He passed away at his Highfields home on 23 June 1888.

The first action of the New Year saw a second visit of the season to Attercliffe, with the hosts gaining some degree of revenge for the opening-day loss by securing a draw. It was then time to reopen cross border hostilities with Derbyshire, although it wasn't the usual opponents for Wednesday as they had lost their mainstay, Mr Houseman, who had the temerity to move to St Helens! In their place was a side from the Derby-based Derwent Rowing Club. A crowd of around 700 were inside Bramall Lane to see their favourites win 3-1, both Butler brothers netting. A second Myrtle Road game against the 105th Regiment was won and the club's run of victories continued at Broomhall and then Heeley before Wednesday played the return fixture with Derby Derwent, held at the Derby cricket ground. Despite spectators constantly encroaching onto the pitch, the match was played to a conclusion with William Clegg 'putting through' the only goal of the game for the visitors before all parties retired to the local Bell Hotel. The final game of the season, at home to Fir Vale, proved somewhat problematic as the visitors turned up with only five men, but the game still kicked off. However, no further players came to the aid of Wednesday's opponents and a shortened game finished 1-0 to Wednesday before the remaining time was filled with a practice match. Despite athletics days being generally on the wane, the Wednesday sports carnival continued to attract competitors and fans, almost 5,000 attending in 1875, with the club charging sixpence for admission to the ground and a further sixpence for the enclosure (ladies free); it was 2s 6d to enter the bicycle race. This was helped greatly by Wednesday offering some of the best prizes ever seen in the town, thanks to generous donations from members and some expense by Wednesday. The day had returned to its traditional Easter Monday slot, with the event notable for the appearance of Billy Mosforth – an individual who, on the football field, would leave an indelible imprint in the early history of Sheffield Wednesday, Mosforth winning the mile handicap from seven others in a splendid time of 4 minutes 58 seconds. The bicycle race was well attended, with an impressive silver cup on offer for the winner. Several well-known players also competed including Herbert Muscroft, Jack Hunter and William Stacey. The overall day, and the football season in general, was deemed a great success for the Wednesday club as they challenged their rivals for the title of 'top dog' in Sheffield.

The Fixture List Evolves

The club's AGM of 1875 welcomed Arliss West as assistant secretary, with Herbert Muscroft also joining the committee. In addition, a link with Wednesday's distant past was re-established when Sydney Stratford, grandson of founder member of the cricket club William, also joined the committee. The traditional opening game of the new season, against Attercliffe, was a victim of heavy rain so a second team defeat at Exchange Brewery's Rock Street ground officially opened the campaign. A visit to Marsh's Thurlstone Crystal Palace proved the first game for the senior side, and with new man Mosforth in fine form Wednesday recorded a 3-0 win with the newcomer scoring a brace – he was quickly called up by the Sheffield FA and made his first appearance against Birmingham soon after. The club's fixture list for the early weeks of the season was strangely sparse with only three more first team games recorded in the remainder of the calendar year, commencing with a poorly attended draw against Derby Derwent, which kicked off late and was played to a conclusion in almost total darkness. More brilliant play from Mosforth, and great performances from the Butler brothers, helped Wednesday to secure a draw, but only around 150 fans paid for admission – the reason given being that it was the end of the town's 'fair week' and most fans had spent all of their wages.

WALTER FEARNEHOUGH

The family name of Fearnehough was inexorably linked with Wednesday FC for over eighty years, with Walter a playing member of the club in the early 1870s and his son, William, later chairman (1944–53). Born in Sheffield on 15 March 1849, his father, William ran a knife manufacturing business and their relative affluence ensured Walter could receive a privileged education at Eccleshall College. At the age of just seventeen he took over the family business, based on Garden Street, which produced 'bayonet spirals, ledger blades and chaff knives'. The young Walter could be found playing for Wednesday in November 1870 – scoring twice in a win at Broomhall – and would eventually spend six years on the club's committee (1873–79). In 1879 he was appointed club vice president and still held the position when Wednesday achieved league status. Walter famously 'employed' James Lang at his business, and he was also instrumental in the move to Olive Grove while his brother, Whiteley, also served on the Wednesday FC committee for a decade. Walter, a conservative, churchman and freemason, eventually became a club director at Owlerton, but was taken ill with bronchial asthma, and passed away at his Claremont Place home on the final day of 1907, aged fifty-eight. A widower twice, Walter was survived by his three sons who kept the family connection alive. His family's success in business was reflected in the £26,891 left in Walter's estate.

The next opponents for Wednesday were a side called Spital United, which mainly consisted of employees from Chesterfield tobacco manufacturers George Mason & Son. The Myrtle Road fixture also highlighted a longstanding problem with the club's home ground as the road leading to the pitch was literally covered in several inches of thick mud – the local inhabitants having petitioned parliament in the hope of resolving the problem. The game finished level with poor light resulting in the teams dispensing with the half-time interval and just changing ends. The club's final game of the calendar year, a goalless home encounter with Broomhall, saw Jack Hunter in the Wednesday side, although the late arrival of several players meant the game did not kick-off until 3.25 p.m. – one can only speculate how the game reached a conclusion, although the actual kick-off time, in present day, would have been an hour later as British Summertime was only introduced in 1916.

The second half of the 1875/76 season was highly significant as Wednesday played their first ever game against the much celebrated Nottingham Forest team and also travelled outside of England for the first time. The former meeting took place on the second Saturday of the New Year, with Forest, who had previously played matches against Sheffield club Norfolk, arranging games against Wednesday as the club's fame started to spread. There was much anticipation in Nottingham for the fixture, but the vast majority of the sizeable crowd would be disappointed as Wednesday cruised to a splendid 5-0 win. A week later, Wednesday won 3-0 at the Derby Racecourse against the Derwent club, although the game was ruined somewhat by spectators constantly encroaching onto the pitch. The match also saw controversy as, with 20 minutes remaining, the home umpire refused two appeals from

Wednesday, which resulted in two men from the away side walking off the pitch in protest. A trio of home games followed with a win over Attercliffe followed by a bizarre game against old foes Heeley where it was not until half-time had been reached that it was realised that Heeley had only thirteen men to Wednesday's fourteen. The 'Heeleyites' objected and the teams duly started afresh; the away side won a shortened game.

The trio of fixtures concluded with a visit from Thurlstone Crystal Palace, although the away side arrived three players short of their full compliment. Wednesday committeeman Harry Ellis was among the scorers as Wednesday won, although only 45 minutes were played due to the poor condition of the pitch and two match balls bursting during the abridged encounter. A return visit to Nottingham followed, this time to face the Notts Castle Club at Trent Bridge, and Wednesday's exploits against Forest a few weeks earlier ensured a large crowd was in attendance. The game proved a much sterner examination for the away side, but an understrength Wednesday team secured a draw thanks to an equaliser from Beardshaw. It was then time for the return game with Spital – played on a pitch outside the gates of the Chesterfield factory. Wednesday arrived short of three players and had to quickly draft three emergency replacements, although one player quickly retired. Two goals from Hanson secured a 2-1 win for the visitors before the home secretary, Mr Shipley, gave the Wednesday players and officials a guided tour of the factory, explaining how 'pig twist' tobacco was manufactured. Wednesday ended the 1875/76 campaign with two more 'high-profile' fixtures, beginning with the 9-1 thrashing of an understrength Nottingham Forest side with Charles Clegg netting a hat-trick. The final game of the season truly showed the potential of the relatively new sport of association football as Wednesday travelled out of England for the first time to visit Glasgow. Interest in the sport was rapidly growing in Scotland, although Wednesday's opponents, Clydesdale, had only been in existence for four years. The crowd at Kinning Park was nothing short of phenomenal, swelled by the possible appearance of the Clegg brothers, as it was noted that 1,000 ladies and gentleman packed into the grandstand; the overall attendance was estimated at around 17,000 – a huge gate for a game of football in 1876, especially when you consider that the first few finals of the FA Cup struggled to attract more than 3,000 fans. Many thousands were locked out, with some 200 coming to grief 15 minutes into the game when the roof of the shed they were perched upon gave way and they were unceremoniously set crashing to the ground. Thankfully there were no serious injuries, just a few cuts and bruises suffered by the resourceful supporters. The result was almost incidental to the scenes that met Wednesday on that day, although with neither of the Clegg brothers putting in an appearance the blue and white hoops lost 2-0 after an experience of how football could really capture the public's imagination.

SIR WILLIAM EDWIN CLEGG

Born in Sheffield on 21 April 1852, William Clegg left a considerable legacy from both a sporting and public service perspective. His father, William Johnson Clegg, started his own law practice in 1868. William would follow in his footsteps, famously defending notorious Sheffield murderer Charlie Peace in 1879. In the early 1870s, William was living with his parents and five siblings in Eccleshall and had just started to become involved in the relatively new sport of football. His first club was Sheffield FC, and over the years he became a vital part of the local football scene as a regular for Wednesday FC, playing in all the early cup finals that made the club's name. Mainly utilised in defence, William was duly capped by England in March 1873, in only their second international game, and therefore ensured that the Clegg's became the first siblings to ever represent England. In the 1875 edition of *Charles Alcock's Football Annual*, William is described as a 'safe kick and good half back'. He was rewarded with a second cap for his country, against Wales in 1879. By then he was appearing for Sheffield Albion and was forced to retire after injuring his arm in a fixture against Vale of Leven in 1880. He had also played hand lacrosse in his youth, and was appointed vice president when the Sheffield and Hallamshire FA was formed in 1887. Away from sport he was known as the 'uncrowned King of Sheffield' due to his position as the leader of the liberals in the town. He served on the town council from 1895 until 1926 and was Lord Mayor in 1898, in addition to being knighted in 1906, and campaigned on a wide variety of issues from improving the tram system to constructing council housing. He continued to work as a solicitor into the twentieth century, and after leaving public office he concentrated on social and philanthropic work, becoming pro-chancellor of Sheffield University. His two sons followed their father into the law practice – the family firm later merged with a fellow practice and is now part of the modern-day Wake Smith Solicitors. Just before his death at a Sheffield nursing home on 22 August 1932, he commented about his playing days: 'people used to think it was only good football when they knocked a man down and hurt him, and the ball was incidental. If you couldn't take the knock, you didn't play'. When Wednesday was converted into a limited company in May 1899, William was on the first board of directors and he remained linked to the club for his remaining years.

The club's sports day was again well attended despite poor weather, with a packed programme ensuring no fan or competitor had time to draw breath before the scheduled 6.00 p.m. finish. For the first time football was included with the four-a-side final seeing ex-Wednesday attacker William Orton grab the 'golden goal' winner for Exchange, against Fir Vale, after the teams were tied at full time and agreed to play on until one side scored. Winners on the day included Wednesday players Mosforth (120-yard dash and 150-yard hurdles), Anthony (440-yard steeplechase), William Stacey (quarter-mile) and George Cropper (footballers' one-lap race). The club's AGM saw Cawthron leave the committee, after eight years, with one of the most influential figures in the Owls' early history, John Holmes, effectively taking his place. Incidentally, in the 1870s members wishing to play had to inform the club's honorary secretary with subscriptions set at 4s 6d, which also gave members the privilege of competing in the annual sports days – it was just 2s for football alone. If a man didn't pay his subs he would be 'blacklisted', and games were often stopped in order that a player might be asked to show his membership card and receipt.

WILLIAM HEATON STACEY

William Stacey officially took over the captain duties from Johnny Marsh in 1874 – a year after joining the club's committee. After playing his early football with St George's, Bill started appearing for Wednesday around 1872, usually as a back or full-back, and was said to be 'quick on his legs', although his kicking was not as sure as other players. He was a regular competitor in the Wednesday athletics days, winning several sprint races, and was generally considered one of the best players in 1870s Sheffield – he also occasionally appeared for Hallam FC. Born in Sheffield in 1848 to dentist father John and mother Elizabeth, Stacey spent his early years at St George's School before studying teaching in Liverpool. He returned home to become a schoolmaster at Broomhill and was subsequently headmaster of the boys' department of the Darnall National School for twenty-five years. He was captain as Wednesday rose to prominence in the 1870s and appeared on several occasions for the Sheffield FA. Although not generally regarded as a goalkeeper – unlike his brother Fred – Bill actually played twice between the sticks in FA Cup football for Wednesday. After retiring he became a noted referee, refereeing the Scotland versus Wales match in March 1898, but became ill late in 1902 and was eventually admitted to a nursing home on Clarkegrove Road. On 5 November 1903 he passed away aged fifty-five; the cause of death was recorded as haemorrhage of the lungs and dropsy.

Cup Football Returns to Sheffield

In the late 1860s both the Youdan and Cromwell cups were competed for in Sheffield, but it was not until 1876 that the Sheffield FA followed the lead of the London FA (FA Cup) by introducing their own knock-out competition, the Sheffield Challenge Cup, with a £50 silver trophy offered for competition by clubs of the 'town and neighbourhood'. The SFA had offered a prize of £5 to design the trophy, with art student F. Fidler submitting the winning design. Wednesday, who now boasted a membership of 230, were one of the favourites for the new trophy in that inaugural season and played the first tie in the competition, in October 1876, when Parkwood Springs were beaten 3-1 at Myrtle Road. The summer had seen Henry Stratford (son of William) join the club's committee, and the new season opened on the first Saturday of October with a surprise 4-0 loss at Attercliffe. After progressing in the new cup, Wednesday put five goals past Spital at Myrtle Road, and a draw at Hallam was significant as not only did James Lang appear in a Wednesday shirt for the first time, but captaining the opposition was Bob Gregory, a player who would later play a significant role for Wednesday – the contemporary match report also included the following evocative line: 'and a good deal of shuttlecock playing took place with the players' craniums, but the sphere was got away at a critical moment'.

The appearance of Lang in a Wednesday shirt was also highly significant as he is believed to be the first Scot to cross the border to play football professionally, although none of Wednesday's officials admitted so, as he was employed by committeeman Walter Fearnehough at his business. However, it later emerged that Lang's responsibilities only involved drinking tea and reading the newspapers, so he was in fact the first instance of veiled professionalism years before the practice began in Lancashire. Further progression followed in the Sheffield Cup: Kimberworth was beaten 1-0, while Wednesday fans had the rare privilege of seeing their side play on Boxing Day with Derby Town providing the opposition at Myrtle Road. Unfortunately the visitors arrived with three men short, and after recruiting from the watching spectators promptly lost 5-1 to Wednesday on a snow covered pitch. New Year's Day saw Wednesday in Sheffield Cup quarter-final action against Attercliffe at their Shirland Lane ground.

The snow of a few days earlier had given way to persistent rain, with the hosts asking for the game to be abandoned at half-time as both players and fans were soaked to the skin. However, Wednesday played on and during the second period the 'sturdy' Frank Butler received a round of applause after barging an opponent into a pool of water. The game did reach its conclusion with a solitary goal from Lang securing passage to the last four for the blue and white hoops (their kit of choice as per Sheffield FA 1877 records). The win over Attercliffe was also significant as it was the first reported instance of a match referee being in charge of a Wednesday game – the forerunner of today's man in the middle first appearing around 1874 in association football. Eventually, around 1891, the referee would be given sole charge of events on the field of play, with the old style umpires becoming modern day assistant referees.

THOMAS AND FRANCIS MOORE BUTLER

The Butler brothers were associated with Wednesday FC during the 1870s, with older brother Francis, born in Rotherham in 1849, first appearing around 1870. Nicknamed 'Little Frank', he stood only 5 feet 4 inches tall and was a real character that held the role of 'pusher through' on the pitch. This meant he effectively hung around the goal hoping to force the ball home, usually along with an opposition player into the bargain – he would stand and chat with his prospective victim until the ball came within reach and then battle began! He was decidedly bow-legged, but was described as the 'most extraordinary little player and when once seen will never be forgotten'. Brother Tom – Sheffield born in 1854 – first appeared for the club in the mid-1870s, and both brothers played, and scored, as Wednesday won the Sheffield Cup in 1877. They helped the club retain the trophy a year later, and also played for Garrick, Mackenzie and Broomhall. They also spent time on the club's committee with Tom serving from 1874– 80 and his brother from 1880–84, regularly helping out on athletics days in the early 1880s.

A defeat followed at Trent Bridge, against Nottingham Forest, with the hosts increasing their admission prices for the visit of the 'famous' Sheffield side. Wednesday 'keeper Fred Stacey returned north with one tooth less after it was kicked out in a scuffle; all was forgotten as the teams retired to the Maypole Hotel for dinner and drinks. A week later, a meeting with Heeley proved eventful as the game was briefly held up during the second half when several youthful spectators ran across the Myrtle Road pitch so they could get a better view of a fight that had broken out between a supporter from each team – crowd disorder evidently not being confined to modern matches. Throughout the game the partisan visiting fans also 'cat-called' Wednesday's best player Lang and there were derisive cheers when he 'came to grass' during the encounter. Nottingham Forest completed a quick-fire double a week later, but all eyes in local football were firmly fixed on the semi-finals of the Sheffield Cup due to be played at Bramall Lane on the first Saturday of February. A tremendous crowd of 6,000 attended the semi-final day, and, after Heeley had beaten Providence, huge cheers went up from the spectators when Wednesday entered the field to face Exchange. Both Clegg brothers were back in the side and Charles hit a post early on before finding the net in a 3-1 win with a brace from Bishop ensuring a place in the final. It was 'after the Lord Mayor's Show' a week later as Attercliffe won at Myrtle Road while, due to no Sheffield ground being available on Shrove Tuesday, a third meeting with Nottingham Forest was switched to Trent Bridge. Wednesday got back to winning ways while goals from Frank Butler and Tomlinson secured a 2-1 win against Derby Town on a sunny winter's day at the South Derbyshire Cricket Ground on Nottingham Road, Derby.

HENRY HAWKSLEY

Sheffield-born on 3 May 1835, Henry Hawksley was a significant figure in the early history of Wednesday FC. He was associated with the cricket club for many years and served as a town councillor. He first joined the cricket club committee in 1865, and in 1868 was elected vice president of both football and cricket sections. He started his working life as a file cutter, but eventually became a hatter, with premises on High Street. Henry was known to have an obliging and friendly deposition, and in 1870 replaced Frank Chambers as president of both sporting sections of 'good old Wednesday'. Twice married, Hawksley played occasionally for the football team in the early 1870s and was a much respected figure on the Sheffield sporting scene, serving as president for seventeen years. Ailing health meant he took a less active role in club affairs from the mid-1880s onwards, and he passed away on 8 May 1887 while still the serving president of Wednesday, leaving a widow and three young children. At a specially convened meeting of SWCC, newly appointed president Henry Stratford sent the club's condolences to his widow Sarah, with the scheduled game against Glossop postponed as a sign of respect.

It was then time for the biggest football match to be played in the town of Sheffield since the sport commenced in the late 1850s, when Bramall Lane hosted the inaugural final of the Sheffield Challenge Cup. The opponents for Wednesday – who uniquely included three sets of brothers in their line up – were the 'auld enemy', Heeley, and a crowd fitting for such an important event, estimated at 8,000, kept the turnstiles clicking up to kick-off, although many gained entry through more unofficial methods. It was noted that the private enclosure at the ground was fuller than it had ever been for a football match with a record attendance of females – an astonishing number of who claimed to be girlfriends or friends of the players, which is surely the first instance of a modern-day WAG!

F. Stacey, W. Stacey, J.C.Clegg, W. E. Clegg, W. Muscroft, E. Buttery, F. M. Butler, T. M. Butler, J. Bingley, J. J. Lang, W. E. Skinner and T. Bishop.

A blow for Wednesday was the absence of star player Mosforth, and this fact seemed to be crucial as Wednesday reached the interval 3 goals in arrears. The cause seemed lost, but with the wind in their favour Wednesday quickly pulled a goal back as Frank Butler converted a Bishop centre. Soon after, Tom Butler scored and suddenly the cup was 'up for grabs' with man of the match 'Little Frank' duly supplying the assist for William Clegg to equalise. Wednesday were denied a late winner when a Heeley player stopped the ball from crossing the line with his hand – no penalty kicks in those days – so time was called with the teams deadlocked after a 3-3 thriller. As a gala dinner, at the Imperial Hotel, was arranged for afterwards, and the expectant crowd wanted to see a conclusion, both teams met in the centre of the field and decided to play a maximum of 30 minutes extra, with the first side to score declared the winner. The match remained deadlocked at the end of the first half of additional time, and with the wind against them, Wednesday were forced to defend stoutly in the second period. However, as the game looked set to heading for a replay, Wednesday broke away and Bishop, who was celebrating his twenty-first birthday, crossed for Bill Skinner to gleefully turn the ball home and win the cup for his side. In the 'dressing stand', Wednesday captain Bill Stacey called for three cheers for Heeley captain Deans, which was vigorously adhered to, before all parties retired to the post-match celebration. Match referee, and President of the Sheffield Association, Mr Shaw, later presented the cup and medals to the Wednesday players, commenting that,

> The association were desirous of cultivating and encouraging the highest and best principles of the noble winter pastime. They were convinced that football, so far from being the deteriorating effect upon the minds of the multitude, which so many of our so-called 'sports' undoubtedly

had, was in a very large degree useful as a moral agency - cultivating as it did gentlemanly habits, good temper, coolness, self-denial, courage and abstemiousness. The association desired that the rules of football should be improved and consolidated from time to time that before long there might be one general code throughout the country.

The last line of that noble speech proved significant as soon after the Sheffield FA agreed with the Football Association to end 'Sheffield Rules' and the game of football started to be played under one standard set of rules that would evolve over time and continue to do so today. The handsome cup was then filled with champagne and passed around, with both team captains taking the first sips. For all of the players it was their first experience of receiving a tangible reward for their deeds on the football field, each receiving silver medals in the shape of the Maltese Cross, enclosed in a 'handsome' leather case, which were to be worn in future matches as a 'distinguishing badge of meritorious play'. The gathering ended late into the evening with the Wednesday men then retiring to their clubhouse on Norfolk Street where birthday boy Bishop was 'baptised' with champagne.

JAMES JOSEPH LANG

James Lang is widely regarded as the first Scottish footballer to travel south to specifically play football. He had made his name in his native country and was first spotted by Wednesday officials when he appeared for Glasgow in February 1876 meeting with the Sheffield FA. Within months he had crossed the border and was handed a job in a business owned by club official Walter Fearnehough, which was just a thin veil to disguise that Lang was effectively the club's first full-time professional, many years before it was legalised. Before joining Wednesday, Lang, born 15 May 1851 in Glasgow, had worked at John Brown's shipyard on the Clyde where, in 1869, he actually lost the sight in his left eye after an accident – it was a fact that Lang kept quiet during his career so no opponent could gain an advantage. Lang, known as 'Jimmy' or 'Reddie', returned home soon after helping Wednesday win the Sheffield Challenge Cup, but returned in 1879 after being capped twice by Scotland, and subsequently appeared in the club's first FA Cup tie. Described as a very skilful forward, possessing great energy and power, Lang only played sporadically for Wednesday from 1882 onwards and eventually signed professional terms at Burnley in 1886. After retiring he returned to Scotland, and in 1901 was a widower living with his four children and working as a boilermaker.

Wednesday still had one game left to play. The match at Spital Chesterfield was tinged with sadness as it also served as a benefit game for the widow and children of the late John Rodgers, who had died just before Christmas. A goal from Charles Clegg earned the away side a draw, with receipts from the estimated crowd of 600 raising much needed funds for Rodgers' family. Just over a fortnight later, Wednesday held their tenth annual sports day to formally bring the curtain down on the 1876/77 campaign. The day was again held at Bramall Lane on Easter Monday, and Wednesday again offered some prizes of 'considerable value', which attracted another healthy crowd. President Hawksley acted as official starter, with Walter Fearnehough (who finished second in the 120-yard handicap race), Chambers and Hill assisting as judges and clerk of the course respectively. Mosforth came first in the hurdles race before runner-up Cawthron was declared the winner after Mosforth was judged to have hit one of the hurdles. The four a-side football competition included Exchange, Heeley, Albion and Hallam, with several players of Wednesday affiliations appearing in the mini tournament including the Clegg brothers, Anthony, Tom Buttery, Mosforth and Gregory. The final between Exchange and Albion ended without a score; the prize was shared. The sports day was now firmly established as the best in the town and helped greatly in cementing Wednesday Club as the premier all-round sports club in the area. There was one last hurrah for the season when Wednesday held their tenth anniversary dinner at the Adelphi, with the Cromwell and Sheffield Cups proudly on display – official Holmes also sportingly presented all the players with pocket knives to commemorate their cup success.

GEORGE ANTHONY

Born in Sheffield on 3 January 1852, George Anthony first appeared for the club in 1870 and represented a variety of teams in that decade including Hallam, Exchange, Norfolk and Broomhall. George, known by his nickname of Nudger, was described as a small, clever and tricky player who was a good dribbler but lacked pace. A table knife grinder, he did not really become a first team regular at Wednesday until the late 1870s, winning the Wharncliffe Cup in 1879 before making a 'competitive' scoring debut in the 2-0 FA Cup win at Providence in November 1881. He would appear in a total of five 'English Cup' ties, scoring three times, although he usually played 'second fiddle' to the incomparable Bob Gregory. His final appearance came in a friendly against the Surrey club in April 1883. He only lived until the age of forty-eight, passing away in June 1900.

A New Ground as Wednesday Start to Dominate Local Football

The game of football continued to grow in the town, and in the industrial north generally, with the Sheffield FA now boasting twenty-six clubs: Albion, Artillery and Hallamshire Rifles, Attercliffe, Brightside, Brincliffe, Broomhall, Crookes, Exchange, Exchange Brewery, Fir Vale, Gleadless, Hallam, Heeley, Kimberworth, Millhouses, Norfolk, Norfolk Works, Owlerton, Oxford, Parkwood Springs, Philadelphia, Rotherham, Sheffield, Surrey, Thursday Wanderers and Wednesday. In addition, the SFA would soon have a rival as the Sheffield New Association was formed on 28 March 1878 in protest against the ruling body's decision to not allow any clubs into their membership who were less than two years old; teams who joined included Attercliffe Zion & Owlerton Broughton, but none of the newcomers showed any longevity. Sheffield would have two ruling bodies for a decade, which caused a decisive split in the town and without doubt diluted Sheffield's influence at the FA, before the 'upstart' new association was absorbed in 1887 to create the Sheffield & Hallamshire FA. The summer of 1877 saw new men voted onto Wednesday's committee: John Vessey, player Jack Bingley and future club secretary James Hoyland. A few weeks into the new campaign the club's supporters would have a new ground to call their own as Wednesday said goodbye to Myrtle Road, moving a few hundred yards to the Sheaf House grounds.

The new season was kicked off by captain Stacey at Attercliffe, who included well-known burlesque actor Fred Vokes in their line-up, with the home side triumphing thanks to a single goal. A week later, Exchange held Wednesday to a draw at their Quibell's Field ground before a goalless encounter with Heeley signalled the end of the Myrtle Road era. Goals from Anthony and Frank Butler then helped to secure a win at Endcliffe before Wednesday had to send a weakened team to Derby due to several players being called up for a Sheffield FA fixture (no games called off due to call ups in those days). Captain Stacey was also out due to 'lameness', and with Harry Ellis taking the armband Wednesday lost 6-0 at the Racecourse Ground.

SIR JOHN CHARLES CLEGG

Like his brother, Charles Clegg left a huge impression on public and sporting life. He shared the same football qualities as William and was described in 1876 as 'one of the fastest forwards to have ever kicked a ball and is a most unerring shot at goal'. The pair were virtually inseparable in the 1870s, mainly representing Wednesday but also appearing for the likes of Norfolk, Sheffield FC, Broomhall and Albion. He was capped by England in their first international, although he later said his colleagues were 'snobs from the south who had no use for a lawyer from Sheffield'.

Charles followed in the footsteps of his father, who had prepared claims for victims of the 1864 Sheffield flood, and qualified as a solicitor in 1872 working alongside his brother in the family practice. He was in the Sheffield FC side that became the first from the town to appear in the FA Cup and played in all Wednesday's big games in the decade, earning various winners medals. Years later he reminisced about the early days of the club, commenting that he had to change behind a hedge and give a local boy a few pennies to look after his clothes.

As a youngster he was also a fine runner, but it was for his off the field achievements that he became known as the 'Napoleon of football'. Among the many posts he held was Chairman of the FA (1890– 23), President of the FA (1924–37), Chairman of Wednesday FC (1915–31), Chairman of Sheffield United (1899–1936), and President of the Sheffield and Hallamshire FA (1887–1937). When he was chairman of both Sheffield clubs he would often hold board meetings on the same night, with United's affairs dealt with briefly before dashing across town to Owlerton. Away from football he served for ten years on the town council and worked as the official receiver for Sheffield. He was also a formidable character, typical of the tough northern Nonconformist, professional liberals that came out of Victorian society, and he was also strictly against alcohol, tobacco and gambling, claiming that 'nobody ever got lost on a straight road' and that if sport remained totally amateur then it could not be corrupted by 'filthy lucre'. He later became a top referee, officiating in the 1882 and 1892 FA Cup finals. He was a man who counted the King of England as a personal friend and in 1927 became the first individual to be knighted for services to football, although the honour was officially for 'services to the Board of Trade and the Ministry of Labour'. He lived to the grand age of eighty-seven, passing away on 26 June 1937 in Sheffield. A memorial was erected in the Wednesday boardroom to honour the man who gave so much to the game of football, both locally and nationally.

A week later the club played their first fixture at their new home, with visitors Exchange Brewery being considered unfortunate to be drawn at holders Wednesday in the Sheffield Cup. The victory in the competition no doubt played a factor in the club's move to the larger Sheaf House grounds, which became the club's fourth home inside ten years. The name of the venue derived from the large house built by Daniel Brammall back in 1816. The sports ground was subsequently developed to the rear of the property, which was effectively sited between modern day Bramall Lane and Shoreham Street, behind the Sheaf House public house. The venue was also an occasional home for Yorkshire County Cricket Club. Wednesday, with the Clegg brothers and Stacey back in their ranks, christened their new home with a 5-0 win. Another visit to the tobacco works was next, an understrength Wednesday side winning 1-0, while games on Boxing Day were still relatively rare. However, Wednesday fans were in luck in 1877 as Derby were hosted at Sheaf House on a snow covered pitch. In fact, it snowed heavily throughout the game and there was a quick turnaround at half-time to ensure the match, which Wednesday won, was concluded.

TOM CAWTHRON

Although born in Dewsbury in 1839, Tom Cawthron was forever known as 'Barnsley Tom' by Sheffield football followers due to his early years spent in the town with his parents and nine siblings. Cawthron was a keen participant in both cricket and football, and was a popular forward for Wednesday FC in the late 1860s/early 1870s. He served the football club for eight years (1868–76) and was also a great servant to Wednesday CC, for whom he played for many years and was secretary between 1872 and 1874. A successful businessman – he owned the Devonshire Engineering works on Egerton Street – Tom took the honour of highest individual score at the cricket's club's fiftieth anniversary dinner in 1870 and remained connected with both the summer and winter game until his death late in 1895.

The first match of 1878 was a sobering 5-1 home defeat to Heeley before the club's playing resources were stretched when Wednesday played two games on the same afternoon, hosting a Sheffield Cup third round tie against Hallam – Wednesday had received a bye in round two – and sending a side to Nottingham Forest. The cup tie at Bramall Lane also doubled as a benefit game for former captain Marsh, and his popularity ensured a bumper crowd and a handsome sum raised for the injured beneficiary, described as 'a brilliant exponent of the game and a 'genial, straightforward and honourable member of society'. A strong Wednesday side beat Hallam 2-0, while down in Nottinghamshire, a late goal from Anthony was purely a consolation in a 4-1 defeat. A disappointing home loss to Exchange followed the cup win. Soon after the news broke that Glasgow Rangers were set to play their first ever game outside of Scotland, at Nottingham Forest. As per usual, the Wednesday executive was quick to react and a game was arranged at Bramall Lane. Club secretary Littlehales organised posters to be distributed around the town, and plans went into action to host a Rangers team that had scored an astonishing 226 goals. The 'Scotch' arrived in Sheffield and around 2,000 paid to see if their favourites could put a brake on Rangers' scoring run. A Wednesday side more than matched Rangers, although during the first half the ground was enveloped in dense smoke thanks to the adjoining mortar mill. The game finished 2-1 in the visitors' favour before all parties dined at Mr Garrett's Sheaf House Hotel.

ROBERT GREGORY

Born in Sheffield in 1853, Bob Gregory was a goal-scoring hero to the first generation of Wednesday fans. He started his sporting career with the St George's Club, taking part in their athletics day when aged just sixteen. His first football was also played with that club – alongside the Staceys – and he made such an impression that by the end of 1873 he was an automatic pick for the Sheffield FA. He became captain of Hallam and played with them for the majority of the 1870s before becoming a Wednesday regular late in the decade, although he missed much of the 1879/80 season after his pony and trap were involved in a collision. He first appeared for Wednesday in January 1873, but made only occasional appearances prior to a hugely successful spell when Bob won two Sheffield Cups and three Wharncliffe Cups. He also played in Wednesday's first FA Cup tie, scoring a hat-trick, and would appear in the first seventeen FA Cup fixtures played by Wednesday, netting 14 goals. He was a real 'talisman' attacker and was described as being one of the most sterling forwards of his day, who worked hard, was difficult to knock off the ball and a great dribbler. In 1882, Gregory became the first Wednesday man to score 5 goals in a 'competitive' game, against Spilsby. In 1880, he'd replaced Bill Stacey as captain, and was rewarded with a benefit game in 1883. He earned a living as a bricklayer and his wife Selina bore Gregory six children over a period of just thirteen years. After his playing days with Wednesday ended he returned to Hallam, for whom he played cricket. He passed away on 22 October 1910 – rather fittingly on the morning of the Sheffield derby game at Owlerton.

It was then back to the Sheffield Cup with Derby, the visitors to Bramall Lane, hoping to knock out the holders. What followed was one of the best games of football seen so far at the cricket ground, with Wednesday player Charles Clegg at his 'vigorous' best, charging several visiting players onto the cinder track that ran around the pitch. The crowd was treated to an extra 30 minutes play after neither side could 'put through' in normal time. Wednesday went ahead with a corner struck by the aforementioned Clegg, which went straight in. Bishop clinched a 2-0 victory, with newcomer 'Chas' Stratford (grandson of club founder William) named man of the match for Wednesday. Forty-eight hours later, Wednesday drafted in former Hallam secretary and player, Albert Slowe, and future Wednesday secretary Harry Pearson for the visit to fierce rivals Heeley, but an understrength away side lost 1-0.

The second final of the Sheffield Cup was played just a week after the semi-final, and it was back to Bramall Lane with long-time rivals Attercliffe the opponents in the 'blue ribbon' event of the local football calendar. Heavy rain the day before meant the playing surface was slippy, but brilliant sunshine lit up the ground when Stacey kicked off for Wednesday. The holders were ahead early, an effort from Frank Butler just creeping over the line. Early in the second period Butler hit the crossbar. Soon after, however, the cup was effectively won when Bishop's long-range effort went through. The clean sheet in the 2-0 success ensured Wednesday had lifted the trophy without conceding a goal, and the Sheffield FA's coffers were greatly boosted with receipts of £77, 10s and 3d. The post-final dinner saw the winners presented with silver medals with gold centres, while the losers each received a new jersey – a gift from SFA president and founder of Hallam FC, John Shaw. Another successful season on the football field ended with a victory at Nottingham Forest, before Wednesday won 3-1 at Spital United, in a charity game to raise funds for the Chesterfield and North Derbyshire Hospital.

ARLISS WEST

Greengrocer Arliss West was born in the Lincolnshire village of Laceby in 1830, but spent the vast majority of his life in Sheffield running his business from premises on Grimesthorpe Road. He was appointed as Wednesday Football Club's honorary assistant secretary – to William Littlehales – in 1875 and served the club for seven years in that capacity before Herbert Muscroft took over the role. A family man who married Caroline in 1856, Arliss had ten children including two sets of twins, but sadly the two boys that bore his forename both tragically died before they reached the age of five. Despite running his own business, it was thought that Arliss could not actually write – he was recorded as making his 'mark' on official documents. In 1866 he received a 5*s* fine, with 4*s* costs, after his weighing scales were found to be deficient despite having been warned earlier about his conduct. Despite this, he was again found guilty of the same offence in December 1867. He did, however, remain a greengrocer for the remainder of his life, avoiding any further trouble with the local authority. He passed away aged around sixty-eight in Sheffield on 29 March 1898.

Before the club members could unpack their cricket whites, there was the still the small matter of the club's eleventh athletics day, which was again held on Easter Monday. Several of the 'old guard' turned out to assist in organising the day – men such as Chatterton and Pilch – while the first secretary of the Sheffield FA, Walter Skinner, also lent a hand in ensuring all ran smoothly. Wednesday player Edwin Buttery won the first heat of the 120-yard handicap race, although crowd favourite Mosforth was forced to pull out due to a rather nasty boil on his back. Also competing was Whiteley Fearnehough, brother of Walter, who would be voted onto the club committee a few weeks later at the AGM. The good crowd enjoyed the events and there was much laughter when virtually the whole field, in the steeplechase, ended up with a soaking after falling into the water.

Football by Electric Light and the Wharncliffe Cup

Wednesday now boasted 300 members at the season opening on the first Saturday of October 1878, with the usual visit to Brightside Lane, Attercliffe. Wednesday included several of their regulars in that first game, men such as Edwin Buttery and Francis Butler, alongside a few newcomers including Peter Patterson. Over 300 fans attended, and it was noted that Mosforth had put on a 'great deal of fat' during the summer and would require some reduction before he returned to the form that had earned him an international reputation. The game finished 1-0 to Attercliffe; Wednesday experienced a poor start as another loss followed, to Heeley at Meersbrook Park. The blue and whites were shorn of the Clegg brothers for that fixture, who had decided to play with the Albion club for the season, and in fact Wednesday fans did not expect a successful campaign as their absence was exacerbated by the loss of both Lang and Bishop. On the following Monday, sporting rivalries were put aside as Bramall Lane played host to a truly innovative event – the first football match under artificial light. The game was staged with the aid of electric light, supposedly the equivalent of 8,000 candles, supplied by Tasker Sons & Co. The personnel of the Reds versus Blues teams were chosen by the Sheffield FA, with the vast majority from Wednesday ranks. A charge of 6d was levied and the crowds flocked to the pitch black cricket ground to see the spectacle close at hand. Success at an athletics meet in London, and on Paris streets, had gained great publicity for Mr Edison's new discovery of electricity, although doubts were raised that it could ever be used in domestic homes. An hour before the advertised start time thousands milled around the ground anticipating the match ahead. Eventual receipts of over £300 suggested around 12,000 people attended the game – the biggest football crowd seen in Sheffield. The lamps and reflectors were initially placed on raised platforms at the corners of the pitch, with two generators placed behind each goal, before the lights were moved to behind the goals, raised some 30 feet into the air. The organisers could not have asked for a more perfect evening and who else but the Clegg brothers captained the teams. It would be the Blues who recorded a 2-0 victory and probably no one inside the ground that night realised they had witnessed a unique moment in the history of the game. After the excitement of electric light, it was back to the regular season with a mixed eleven losing a first meeting with Endcliffe, at Banner Cross, where the final score would have been even more emphatic but for the fine display of Wednesday goalie Fred Stacey. The disappointing start to the campaign continued in the first Sheaf House game as Wednesday were held by visitors Staveley, but the defence of the Sheffield Cup brought the long-awaited first win, as the Oxford Club were beaten. When Wednesday travelled to Abbeydale Road to face the Albion club, it was noted that the home side had improved their ground, having introduced a rope around the pitch. An almost unrecognisable Wednesday side shared 4 goals. Scorer of the opening goal for Albion was Charles Clegg, perhaps reminding Wednesday fans why their side had struggled for any real form.

EDWIN AND TOM BUTTERY

Brothers Edwin and Thomas Buttery immediately entered the club history books when they both appeared in Wednesday's first FA Cup tie, becoming the first siblings to play in a competitive game. The Sheffield-born brothers, Tom in 1852 and Edwin in 1858, started their careers with Millhouses and later in the decade the pair started to occasionally play for Wednesday – both being drafted into the side in 1879 to help Wednesday win the Wharncliffe Cup. Tom worked as a table knife cutter at Lockwood Brothers, based near to his Bramall Lane home, and would primarily play for the works side, still appearing for them into his mid-thirties. Edwin followed in the footsteps of his father by becoming a bootmaker and was considered such an outstanding footballer that he was named as reserve for England – for their game against Scotland in March 1882. He was by then an Exchange player, although he was back in Wednesday colours to win the Sheffield Cup in 1883. Tom appeared in two competitive games for Wednesday, while Edwin played eleven times in the FA Cup, his final game being in the semi-final of the tournament in 1882. The siblings both passed away in Sheffield in 1916.

Unfortunately, the club's fortunes would deteriorate further as, a week later, Wednesday crashed out of the Sheffield Cup at Hallam's Sandygate ground. The hosts included Gregory, and he scored twice as the holders grip on the trophy ended after a 3 0 defeat. On the Monday following the cup exit, Bramall Lane hosted the first game in a new charity cup, donated by Lord Wharncliffe, which bore his name. The magnificent silver trophy was officially handed over to the SFA at the opening match between Heeley and Hallam. The benefactor intended for the cup to be competed for by clubs of the 'town and district' with all proceeds, after expenses, used for charitable purposes. The opening game saw the monies raised given to the Mayor's Relief Fund, which helped to alleviate distress in the town, although the SFA also donated to the fund after the game raised less than expected. Thankfully, the poor opening weeks of the season did eventually give way to much happier times, with a trio of wins recorded during the holiday period, beginning with a home victory over Nottingham Forest. Heavy snow then caused the postponement of the Boxing Day return game against Forest. The first match of the New Year, at home to Albion, was played on a ground thick with snow. Wednesday won 2-0, with Harry Pearson appearing in goal with regular 'keeper Fred Stacey playing outfield. The wintry weather did not abate and the meeting with Thurlstone Crystal Palace was played in a snowstorm. It was then time for cup tie football again as Wednesday were drawn to play Attercliffe, at Bramall Lane, in the semi-final of the new Wharncliffe Cup. However, the day would prove controversial as the club's opponents, after claiming they had not received enough notice to get their best side together, simply refused to play. A game did go ahead though on a pitch 3–4 inches deep in snow – Wednesday losing to a team captained by Mr Beardshaw. At a subsequent Sheffield FA meeting they awarded the tie to Wednesday on the grounds that they had eleven men on the pitch at the start time. Therefore Wednesday reached the final of the new competition without even playing a game!

JOHN HOLMES

Along with Arthur Dickinson, John Holmes was the most influential Wednesday figure of the pre-league period, joining in 1872. He was born in Sheffield on 11 July 1841 and boasted a famous father, Adam, who was a war hero serving under the Duke of Wellington at Waterloo and in the Peninsular Wars, losing his left leg during battle. John became a successful businessman in Sheffield and ran his own cutlery manufacturing business that employed twenty men and woman in 1881. He became an increasingly influential figure at Wednesday during the 1880s, having joined the committee in 1878, and served as vice president between 1879 and 1887. He was credited as the main instigator behind the move to Olive Grove and served as club president from that year until well into the twentieth century. He was once described as 'genuine, thorough and candid with a hearty, ringing laugh and a good old sportsman, full of reminiscences of the early days of Sheffield football – as good a judge of a joke as a football player, or better'. He was a great believer of employing local talent and took a keen interest in all levels of Sheffield football in the hope of uncovering a jewel. He took full part in the training of Wednesday and was still the club 'kingpin' when Wednesday won the FA Cup in 1896 and subsequently moved to Owlerton. He passed away on 28 March 1908 and was buried in the Derbyshire village of Eyam.

After the controversy of the Attercliffe game, Wednesday seemed to revert to their poor form of early season, losing to both Endcliffe and Staveley. A crowd of 500 then watched at Bramall Lane as a rehearsal for the charity cup final saw Heeley record a convincing 4-0 victory. It had been a tough old season for Wednesday fans and they must have despaired as their favourites extended the run of losses to five at Spital Chesterfield where outfield player Housley took a turn 'between the sticks' and it is also believed Harry Winterbottom made his first appearance. A week later, Wednesday fielded only ten players in a defeat at Derby. On the following Monday evening, Winterbottom scored the winner as Exchange Brewery won at Sheaf House. It would be fair to say that Wednesday's form up to the Wharncliffe Final could hardly have been any worse, and the odds were firmly stacked in favour of Heeley for the first final of the season in Sheffield – a club called Thursday Wanderers surprisingly won the Sheffield Cup two weeks later. Around 3,000 fans were inside Bramall Lane for the inaugural final of the new cup. It was Wednesday who started proceedings. Not long after kick-off, Wednesday received a large slice of luck as Heeley 'keeper Moss ran out of his goal to clear the ball but only succeeded in firing it against the legs of attacker Woodcock, from where it rebounded back into the net. The goal gave Wednesday a huge boost and they would dominate the first period, reaching half-time 2-1 ahead after Woodcock netted on the stroke of the interval to restore his side's advantage. Wednesday kicked into a strong wind in the second period, but despite Heeley still being regarded as favourites by the local betting fraternity it was they who extended their lead after Woodcock completed his hat-trick. It was effectively game over with Heeley scoring a mere consolation goal in the dying embers of the game as Wednesday secured the first Wharncliffe Charity Cup. After a season of struggle, victory in the competition ensured Wednesday had lifted silverware in three consecutive campaigns, and, despite winning only five games all season, could still rightly lay claim to being the town's best team, mainly thanks to one outstanding display against Heeley. Before the end of the season, the Wednesday club announced that they would be holding a four a-side tournament at the Sheaf House Grounds, with four silver watches to the winning side and four gold lockets to the runners up. Twelve teams entered the competition, which was played over two days, and it was Hallam, containing Gregory and Mosforth, who walked away with the bounty after beating Exchange 3-0 in the final.

ARTHUR MALPASS

It's believed that Arthur Malpass was born in Rotherham around 1855 and started his football career at Attercliffe, playing alongside his brother Charles. After playing for Exchange he became attached to Wednesday, first appearing for them in 1877, and became an automatic choice in defence after becoming a Wednesday man in 1879. He served on the Wednesday committee (1879–83) and, as well as earning several local honours, was one of the eleven men who played in the club's first FA Cup tie. He appeared in a total of fifteen FA Cup games for Wednesday, although he was barred from an 1883 tie after Nottingham Forest protested that Arthur had received 30s to play in an earlier fixture. It was not the first time he had been in trouble with the authorities as he was also banned in 1882 after being found guilty of receiving remuneration in the 'Zulu' games. He missed much of his final season at Wednesday through injury before his career took an unlikely twist in 1886 when Malpass – a renowned cricketer for Mexborough – was engaged to play for the Carlton Cricket Club in Edinburgh. He seemingly settled in Lancashire and died around 1906 in Bury.

Thoughts had long since turned to cricket when Wednesday held their athletics sports day in 1879, the meeting having been put back to early June. Crowds continued to attend in numbers, 3,000 on this occasion, with entertainment supplied by the Yeomanry Calvary Band. The usual wide array of activities was on offer, with former player George Sampson winning the 120-yard handicap flat race and James Hoyland winning the 150-yard hurdles. Several other members of the Wednesday football side also registered top three finishes including Malpass, Sheel and Housley.

There were big changes behind the scenes during the 1879/80 close season with long-serving vice president Alf Stacey (no relation to Fred or William) resigning his position after seven years, while both Holmes and Walter Fearnehough stepped up from the general committee to join Hill as vice presidents. Also joining the committee were Lang and Malpass as the Wednesday hierarchy swelled to a somewhat cumbersome twenty-six – a figure higher than any previously recorded and one that would fall to just eighteen a year later as the administrational side of the club was streamlined. The new campaign opened at the Newhall Grounds against Attercliffe where Wednesday had to field Tom Butler between the sticks due to the absence of an ill Fred Stacey. Wednesday started the season with a 2-1 victory before losing at Heeley. Regular goalie Stacey was back for two consecutive games at Quibell's Field as Wednesday met Exchange Brewery in a pre-arranged club match before returning a week later to contest a Sheffield Cup tie.

FREDERICK HEATON STACEY

Brother of William, Fred Stacey served on the club's committee for six years from 1874 and was Wednesday's first regular goalkeeper. After initially appearing for St George's FC, he remained Wednesday's first choice for the vast majority of the 1870s, winning many medals including the Sheffield Challenge Cup and Wharncliffe Charity Cup before the advent of Henry Hall. Born in Sheffield in 1853, Fred worked as a timekeeper in an electroplate factory and was a father to three sons and a daughter. He spent all of his working life in Sheffield before passing away, aged sixty-five, in 1918.

Not unlike the previous season, Wednesday were struggling to field a truly competitive eleven – despite the return of Lang – with many of their 'old guard' having failed to commit to representing the club. There were also murmurs of discontent among supporters, which was voiced after Wednesday lost 1-0 in the cup tie against a side that contained Tom Buttery, Winterbottom and Anthony. It was the second season running that Wednesday had exited the Sheffield Cup at an early stage and Wednesday fans were definitely not amused. A victory over Spital, in the first game of the season at Sheaf House, helped to lift spirits, although the appearance of Bishop in the opposition eleven no doubt reminded fans of happier times. Another morale boosting win, at Holmes FC, was followed by a Wharncliffe Cup first round tie against Hallam at Sheaf House. A much stronger Wednesday side, watched by a crowd of 2,000, lived up to their reputation as holders by recording a third win in a row to reach the semi-finals, Charles Clegg scoring in a 2-1 success. On the Tuesday after the cup win, fans of Sheffield football were treated to the rather strange sight of eleven players running around the Bramall Lane pitch dressed as Zulus, wearing black curly wigs, beads and feathers, black make up and grass skirts, while holding shields and Assegai spears. Included in the Zulu side, which was pitched against a local eleven, were several men with Wednesday connections including Dabulamanzi (Hunter), Sirayo (Malpass), Maguenda (Lang), Ngobamalrosi (Woodcock), Muyamani (Anthony) and Cetawayo (Tom Buttery). The occasion was a benefit game for the widows and orphans of the Zulu War, which was being fought in Southern Africa between the British Empire and the Zulus. The war would last less than six months, but the Zulu football team in England would later cause a multitude of problems that would force the issue of professionalism into the open.

The charity side had already played a benefit match at Scarborough and would later play at Chesterfield, touring the town in full costume before the match. It would be a few months before the Zulu controversy rocked Sheffield and English football. Back in club football, it was a case of 'one step forward, two steps back' for Wednesday as they crashed 6-0 at home to Broomhall – the club's worst ever defeat on home soil in their relatively short history. It was clear that Wednesday needed to address their sub-standard senior side but in an era of purely amateur footballers, it was often difficult to bolster ranks as officials could only use their powers of persuasion and players would usually flock to sides that were winning on a regular basis and those that offered good prospects of winning silverware – Wednesday clearly not fitting into either category despite their previous successes.

THOMAS MAHON BISHOP

Tommy Bishop was only connected to Wednesday for a handful of seasons, but he proved a big favourite with those early fans of the club, helping the blue and whites become the dominant force in Sheffield. Born in the town on 10 March 1856, Bishop – nicknamed 'Little Tommy' due his 5-foot 3-inch height – moved to Chesterfield when just eight years old, and a year later (!) gained employment at Mason's Tobacco Factory. He remained in that trade for the rest of his life – working as a tobacco spinner – and made a football name for himself at Spital Chesterfield. Wednesday procured his services in 1876 and Tommy earned the title of 'one of the best outside right wingers' when his mazy run set up the winning goal in the 1877 Sheffield Cup victory. The game was played on his twenty-first birthday and he was carried shoulder high from the field by joyous fans. He helped Wednesday retain the trophy a year later and win the Wharncliffe Cup in 1879 before returning to Spital colours around 1880. He also represented Nottingham Forest and was selected on numerous occasions to represent the Sheffield FA before his playing career came to a close in 1887. He died in Chesterfield at the latter end of 1935, aged seventy-nine.

The tale of woe continued with a loss at Derby, played on a skating rink for a pitch, before a change of tradition resulted in a truly packed fixture list over the Christmas and New Year period. This resulted in the club playing five games, commencing with a home fixture against Endcliffe. The home side were again shorn of several of their best players, including the likes of Lang, Malpass, Bingley and William Clegg, and despite leading 2-0 the visitors forced a draw. The calendar year ended with a defeat at Walsall and draw at Wednesbury Strollers before New Year's Day saw Wednesday back in cup action with a comfortable Wharncliffe Cup semi-final win against Spital Chesterfield at Sheaf House. Wednesday then welcomed highly rated 'Scotch' side Vale of Leven, who were fresh from victory over Blackburn Rovers. A crowd of around 1,500 were inside the ground to welcome the 'Knights of the Thistle', but the game was stopped early on when William Clegg fell awkwardly and badly injured his arm. He was forced to retire and in an act of sportsmanship the visiting side allowed Wednesday to make a substitution – a gesture warmly applauded by supporters and potentially the first instance of a substitution in a senior game.

A well organised visiting team won 3-0 and a single goal defeat, at Banner Cross against Endcliffe, ensured that Wednesday were again in poor form in the run up to the final of the Wharncliffe Cup – simply known in Sheffield as the 'Charity Cup'. Heeley were again in opposition and the match created great interest because although the trophy on offer was less valuable than the Challenge Cup, it was only the best teams in the district who competed as the competition was strictly invitation only. It was Wednesday who started the ball rolling, kicking downhill towards Bramall Lane, and they struck the crossbar early on before Heeley grabbed the lead against the run of play. A second-half equaliser from Hawley put the fate of the cup back in the balance, but a late winner from the Heeleyites took the trophy from Wednesday's grasp and ensured they would end the season 'potless'.

HERBERT NEWBOULD

Herbert Newbould, along with his brother Frederick, were regulars for Wednesday in the early 1880s, with Herbert appearing in their first FA Cup tie a few weeks after making his debut. Sheffield born in 1863,

Herbert would only have been a teenager when he was a regular at Wednesday. The forward became one of the youngest to ever score a 'senior' hat-trick when he achieved the feat against Spilsby Town in 1882, aged just nineteen. He secured both Sheffield and Wharncliffe Cup winners medals in Wednesday colours and also represented the Sheffield FA. He later briefly appeared for Derby St Lukes and served Wednesday FC as a committeeman between 1883–85 and 1891–92 as well as being the club's official auditor between 1890 and 1892. Away from football he worked for Sheffield company Firth Brothers for an astonishing fifty-four years, eventually becoming chief buyer for the firm. His involvement with athletics, and particularly running, arguably left a greater impact than his football career. As a youngster he was a highly rated runner, winning prizes all over the North of England, and the 'notable miler' would become president of prominent Sheffield athletics club Hallamshire Harriers for forty years in addition to serving in the same capacity for the Northern Counties AAA . He was appointed vice president of the National AAA in 1922 and later became one of the association's first life-presidents. He was also a keen cyclist and a member of his local cycling association. Herbert would live to the age of seventy-three before passing away in Worksop in 1936.

Defeats to Eckington Rovers and Nottingham Forest followed before alarm bells rang with club officials when only 200 Wednesday fans attended the Sheaf House game against Derby on Shrove Tuesday. Only the second win of 1880 came eleven days later when Wednesday hosted the return game with Forest, although the crowd was adversely affected by a big cup tie next door at Bramall Lane. The match also saw the launch of a benefit for club secretary Littlehales, with Wednesday glad to receive any donations towards his fund. A goal after just 3 minutes from Gregory was enough to secure a much needed victory, but a week later the club was humiliated at Staveley where another understrength side was crushed 7-0.

Not unlike the previous campaign, Wednesday fans were probably wishing the season was already over, although one of the remaining two games did at least produce a win – at Spital in a charity game for the Chesterfield and North Derbyshire Hospital – before Staveley completed a quick-fire double with a final day victory at Sheaf House. Football for the season at Wednesday's home ended a fortnight later when the club hosted their second four a-side medal competition, again offering silver watches and gold lockets as prizes. Eight sides entered: Wednesday, Heeley, Ecclesfield, Pyebank, Providence, Spital, Exchange and Albion – the last named failing to appear on the day. The no show by Albion gave Exchange a bye to the semi-finals. Wednesday beat Pyebank and then Spital (containing Tommy Bishop) to earn a final meeting with Heeley. A Wednesday side containing Lang, Malpass, Tom Buttery and Stacey, fought hard in the final, but eventually lost 1-0 to their fierce rivals.

The club's athletics sports day was back in its usual Easter Monday slot and was well attended with almost £100 taken at the turnstiles to swell the club's coffers – the proceeds equated to around £11,000 today and for a purely amateur club the yearly event was a considerable aid to cash flow, particularly in the early years of Wednesday's history when it was difficult to take a gate at their home venues, with the exception of the big games played at Bramall Lane.

The usual array of helpers made the afternoon run smoothly. Wednesday decided to run exactly twelve events, commencing with a 120-yard handicap flat race. The steeplechase saw Wednesday members take the first three positions – Whiteley Fearnehough, Mosforth and Malpass – while Lang took the first prize in the 880-yard handicap flat race. The organisation of the event was once again of a high standard and ensured the sports day remained the best event of its kind in the town. A week later, in May 1880, it was Wednesday who let another club organise the day as they entered a four a-side football team in the athletics day of the Chesterfield Club. The strong Wednesday side containing Bishop, Bill Stacey, Lang and Gregory rather unsurprisingly walked away with the honours, beating Devonshire, Dronfield Exchange and Clay Cross in the final of the 5 minutes each way tournament.

FA Cup, Back to Winning
Ways and Zulu Troubles

The club's AGM in the summer of 1880 resulted in long-serving Bill Stacey moving into a vice president role and Mosforth voted onto the club's commitee, while Gregory was voted as the club's new team captain, replacing Stacey. However, perhaps the biggest news was the club's application, and acceptance, to enter the 'English Cup' for the first time. Wednesday fans hoped for a better season after two campaigns of relative struggle, and thankfully the early 1880s saw Wednesday bounce back in style to re-establish their position as the best team in Sheffield and also to forge a fine reputation outside of local football. The new season opened with the traditional curtain raiser at Attercliffe where the game kicked off nearly an hour late and with neither side at full strength. The opening encounter finished 0-0, but the appearance of Tom Cawley for the home side proved significant as he made such an impression on Wednesday officials that he was almost immediately recruited.

HERBERT AND WILFRED MUSCROFT

Born in the early 1850s, Herbert Muscroft was connected to Wednesday for twenty-five years, from playing for the club in the 1870s to serving behind the scenes until the early 1890s. A blade grinder, Herbert mainly played football for his works side – Joseph Rodgers & Sons – and would often appear alongside his brother Wilfred. He also served on the club's committee (1875–82), was assistant secretary (1882–85) and was again a committee man from 1886 onwards. Herbert married his wife Anne in 1874, but tragically lost three daughters before they had reached two years of age. Muscroft started to ail in 1898 and died of dropsy (oedema) on 27 December 1898, in his forty-eighth year. His brother Wilfred, born early in 1858, was a noted player for Wednesday, appearing in the 1877 Sheffield Cup win. He made the headlines for the wrong reasons in

October 1888 when he was charged with assaulting a railway porter after he had travelled to watch Wednesday play at Nottingham Forest, and was fined 20s at a police court. At the time he was employed by Wednesday secretary Harry Pearson in the silver industry and it was probably that link that secured Wilfred the role of Wednesday trainer in the late 1880s. He was in charge of the team for the 1890 FA Cup final, supervising 9-mile walks around Matlock Bath and an hour's ball work every day, but his service was unexpectedly terminated by Wednesday in January 1892. He passed away on 8 February 1915.

The club played their first home game, against Heeley, at Bramall Lane after the ground committee agreed to rent the enclosure to both Wednesday and Sheffield FC for the 1880/81 season – this probably being the main reason why Wednesday virtually deserted their Sheaf House home, only playing a solitary game there. The entry into the FA Cup was probably a reason behind the decision as the club could not charge for admission at the relatively basic surroundings of Sheaf House, which was also much smaller than the Bramall Lane Cricket Ground. The aforementioned opening game at Bramall Lane ended 4-2 to a Wednesday side that on paper looked to be much stronger than twelve months earlier, with Lang, Mosforth and Gregory all scoring and men such as Edwin Buttery and Chas Stratford in the team. Six goals were then shared at a rain soaked Bramall Lane with Staveley, although Wednesday conceded a 3-1 advantage. Incidentally, the blue and whites also included Heeley regular Peter Andrews in their line-up – a left winger who is generally recognised as the first ever Scottish player to cross the border to play in England. However, unlike his countryman Lang, it was his job that took him to Leeds in 1876. A trip to Exchange was next on the agenda, the unbeaten start continuing with a 2-1 victory. It was then time for the Sheffield Cup and Wednesdayites hoped that their side would avoid the somewhat meek exits suffered in the previous two seasons. The draw took Wednesday to Crookes-based club White Cross FC, and the two-time winners dominated from the start on a pitch that was so small the ball was constantly going out of play. Wednesday duly registered a comfortable win before the club's unbeaten start to the campaign looked in jeopardy when Wednesday invited Glasgow club Queens Park to Bramall Lane. The famous amateur club were widely recognised as the 'champion club' of Great Britain, with their side containing seven of the Scotland team that had recently faced England. It was commented that is was somewhat presumptuous of a provincial club (Wednesday) to challenge the might of the 'Scotch' side, but it must have been disappointing for club officials when the match failed to attract the expected audience, only around 500 coming through the Bramall Lane turnstiles, although the game being played on a Thursday afternoon was a major factor. Those that did attend witnessed a masterclass from the visitors, who won 5-0 in a game where the still-to-be-unified rules resulted in the Scottish 'square' throw-in used in the first half and the English system of throwing the ball in any direction, used in the second period. Their visit proved ironic as the FA Cup draw paired the teams together in the first round of the competition in Sheffield – Scottish teams entered until 1887 when they were banned by the Scottish FA. The tie though was never played as the Scots scratched from the tournament, as they did in previous and subsequent years, giving Wednesday a walkover.

It was commonplace in those days for teams to withdraw, especially if a tie involved a long trip, with five doing so in the 1880 first round. However, before Wednesday could prepare for a tough second round tie at renowned cup fighters Blackburn Rovers, there was the small matter of eight more fixtures to fulfil, commencing with a stalemate against Exchange. A comfortable 4-0 win at the County Ground, Derby, followed before a first meeting with Phoenix Bessemer in the second round of the Sheffield Cup. Wednesday were strong favourites for the tie and many in the press thought the game was a 'foregone conclusion' – an opinion probably shared by the Sheffield football watching public as only 300 paid for admission. The plucky underdogs were 2-1 in arrears at the break, but Wednesday then powered away to eventually win 8-1, with Gregory grabbing 4 goals. A repeat of the previous season's charity final was then staged at Bramall Lane, with Wednesday and Heeley meeting in the semi-finals. The tie ended 2-2, and a week later fans returned for what many believed was the replay. However, it transpired that the game was merely a friendly with Charles Pilling (borrowed from White Cross FC) scoring twice as a strong Wednesday XI won 5-2. A draw at Walsall Town preceded the Sheffield Cup tie against Providence, which saw a new rule come into force when just before half-time Mosforth watched his effort on goal pushed over the bar by a defender's hand. Wednesday appealed and under the new rules the umpire awarded a goal to the blue and whites – Wednesday eventually won 7-0. Both Exchange and Wednesday then met at Bramall Lane, with lots of younger players being given a 'trial spin', and it was the latter who extended their excellent start to the season with an eighth win in fourteen games.

Thoughts now turned to the FA Cup and a trip to face a Blackburn Rovers side that just over a year later would become the first 'provincial' club to reach the final. The hosts were favourites with the pundits, particularly as they had been blessed with a home draw. The Wednesday eleven who lined up on that famous day at Alexandra Meadows were as follows:

W.H. Stacey (gk), T. Buttery, E. Buttery, J. Hunter, J. Hudson, A. Malpass, H. Winterbottom, J. J. Lang, W. Mosforth, H. Newbould and R. Gregory (capt.)

HARRY EYRE PEARSON

Attercliffe-born Harry Pearson (7 August 1851) was a great lover of both cricket and football, playing and following both sports enthusiastically. It's believed he became a member of Wednesday in 1872 and played both sports for the club in the 1870s. He was a right arm pace bowler and eventually progressed to play four first-class games for Yorkshire between 1878 and 1880, taking five wickets for 79 runs (best figures 4-37 versus Surrey) and scoring 21 runs. For the remainder of his cricketing career he played mainly for Yorkshire's Colts side, as captain, and for Wednesday. He had initially joined the cricket club committee in 1877 and between 1884 and 1889 was not only a player but also club secretary – he was also secretary of the football section for three years between 1888 and 1891, preceding Arthur Dickinson. In the final game of the 1888 cricket season he grabbed seven wickets including a hat-trick, and scored 35 to reaffirm his status as the club's best player. He was captain of the Wednesday CC 1st XI in 1889 and continued to play cricket into the twentieth century, only retiring in 1901. Harry was a keen attendee of Yorkshire CCC games at Bramall Lane, but after watching his county play Surrey he suffered a serious stroke and passed away at the age of fifty-one on 8 July 1903.

Match day saw a hard frost cancel all rugby games in the Manchester area, but thankfully the hardness of Rovers' pitch was relieved somewhat by a heavy fall of rain around noon. It was not an ideal day for the estimated 2,000 fans either as snow and rain fell throughout the match, causing great discomfort to all concerned. It was Gregory who kicked off the club's story in the FA Cup, playing into what was described as a 'perfect hurricane', and the story of the game centred mainly around the teams respective choice of footwear – Wednesday adopted a kind of leather stud while Rovers fitted strips of felt to the soles of their boots. The vast majority inside the ground were of the opinion that Wednesday had made the wrong choice, but it was Rovers who could not keep their feet and after a goalless first half the visitors 'skated' to a 4-0 win after Gregory opened the club's account in the FA Cup, 5 minutes into the second period. The Wednesday attacker ended the afternoon with a hat-trick to his name, with Winterbottom also 'putting through' in a dream start to life in the competition. Wednesday had only one more game to play in 1880 and, by coincidence, it was also against a Blackburn side, but this time at the Hole-i'th-Wall ground – home to Blackburn Olympic. Like their near neighbours, the Blackburn club were history makers in the FA Cup as in 1883 Olympic became the first team from a 'working-class' background to win the trophy, ending the domination of the competition by university and old boys' teams. Wednesday repeated their success of nine days earlier by beating Olympic 3-1 to bring the curtain down on a year that had started badly but ended on a real high note.

JAMES HOYLAND

James Hoyland, born in 1854, was first a member of Wednesday FC back in 1872, aged sixteen, and loyally served for many years as a committee man (1877-91). During the period he also spent two years as club secretary (1883-85) and was described as a 'sportsman of the best type', alluding to his love of all sports including athletics, cricket and football. While studying at Wood's College – an exclusive private Sheffield school – he beat athletics records set by William Clegg and was a regular competitor at Wednesday's sports days, once beating Mosforth. As a footballer, he was an outside right and mainly appeared for Norfolk, Wednesday and Broomhall; in the summer months he appeared for Wednesday Cricket Club. Hoyland, along with Sydney Stratford, is credited with finding Wednesday a new home at Olive Grove. He was also instrumental in electing Arthur Dickinson onto the committee. He served for many years as the secretary of the Sheffield Football Players' Accident Fund – a body that compensated players for loss of earnings – while away from sport he worked as a silver chaser, which was a term used to describe highly creative individuals who made intricate designs on silver by hand. When Bramall Lane was the home of Yorkshire CCC, James became official second team scorer in 1889 before stepping up to the first XI in 1900 – he also became scorer for the England side. The greatly loved Hoyland passed away after a short illness in the Sheffield Royal Hospital on 25 January 1921.

The FA Cup was not kind to Wednesday, with the draw sending them back to Lancashire, to face Turton – a side based near to Bolton. On the day of the tie, Wednesday also had the return game with Walsall Town arranged at Bramall Lane. It was decided to go ahead with both matches, meaning playing resources were severely stretched. Despite the win at Rovers,

Wednesday made several changes to their side, but this had little effect on the final outcome as the blue and whites impressed again 'over the border', with Gregory opening the scoring in a game played in dense fog on a bone hard pitch. A second goal came via Rhodes and Wednesday held off a late revival from the hosts to secure a 2-0 win to join the likes of Aston Villa, Old Carthusians (the eventual winners) and Romford in the fourth round, which bizarrely included twelve teams. Back in Sheffield, a virtual reserve side performed admirably against Walsall, narrowly losing 2-1. A week later, Wednesday faced a new force in Sheffield football – edge tools and knife manufacturers Lockwood Brothers – in the semi-final of the Sheffield Cup, but on a snowy afternoon at Bramall Lane 4 goals from Bingley helped Wednesday to a 7-1 win and a third final in five seasons.

The week that followed proved one of the most turbulent in Sheffield football history as the controversy of the Zulu charity games – and the issue of professionalism – came to a head when at a Sheffield FA emergency meeting a resolution was passed 'that future players taking part in a Zulu match or in any way receiving remuneration from playing be barred from playing in any association contest or cup tie'. It had transpired that the men involved in the Zulu novelty games had been receiving a proportion of the gate receipts and in an age of amateurism this forced draconian action. The men who had already appeared for the novelty side were immediately banned, and it was under this cloud that the delayed semi-final replay of the Wharncliffe Cup took place between Heeley and Wednesday. The Sheffield FA's decision deprived Heeley of Hunter and Moss and Wednesday of Malpass. Before the tie commenced the Heeley secretary handed an official letter of protest to SFA secretary Pierce-Dix. The match ended in a comprehensive 7-2 win for Wednesday – the tie finishing despite a heavy fall of snow – but the Zulu issue would rumble on for several more weeks. Soon after the disputed semi-final, the SFA accepted apologies from the 'Zulu' players and the men were duly re-instated, although association secretary Pierce-Dix was a high profile casualty of the controversy after being wrongly accused of accepting monies for his role with the SFA - he was later cleared and re-instated.

The protest of Heeley was also later upheld and they were allowed back into the tournament although the suggestion put forward that they should face Exchange, to determine who would play Wednesday, came to nothing when Exchange refused the proposal. In the end, when the committee of the Charity Cup met, in late March 1881, they took the only option really available by withdrawing the trophy for the season.

JOHN HOUSLEY

Jack Housley enjoyed a long and distinguished career in local football
in the 1870s and 1880s, commencing with Garrick. He also appeared
frequently for Wednesday, United Mechanics and Hallam, but really made
his name as a player for Exchange and Lockwood Brothers, being capped
several times by the Sheffield FA. During his working life Jack was a
groom and cab driver. His popularity with the Sheffield football fraternity
was shown in 1885 when a benefit match was arranged. It is also believed
he was trainer to Sheffield United, in their first season, and would also
play the occasional game. He later worked as assistant trainer to George
Waller at United and was still occupying that role when he came to an
untimely end on 27 September 1908, aged sixty-four, when alighting from
a tram car. He had the misfortune to tread on a banana skin, suffering
three broken ribs and internal injuries in the subsequent fall. He was
taken to the Royal Hospital but did not survive.

As the dust settled on the turbulent off the field events, Wednesday's
attention again turned to the English Cup and yet another tie over the
Pennines, this time at Darwen, situated in the shadow of Blackburn. The
club had certainly been unlucky to receive three consecutive away draws
in their debut season, and a visit to the Lancashire Cup holders provided
another difficult obstacle. Wednesday reverted back to virtually the side that
had beaten Blackburn, and the fixture created huge interest with hundreds
of fans travelling from the Blackburn and Accrington areas to swell the gate
to between four and five thousand. A hard-fought first half did not trouble
the scorers, but Wednesday were then hit with two quick-fire goals before
Gregory reduced the deficit, only for Darwen to re-establish a two-goal
lead and eventually win 5-2. Outstanding forward Gregory scored the
second for his side and Wednesday bowed out of the competition with
their heads held high, having made a significant first impression. It was
then time to concentrate on the remainder of the season with the next four
games resulting in an incredible goals tally of 34, beginning with a runaway
6-1 victory at Wednesbury Elwell's on a bitterly cold afternoon. Back at
Bramall Lane, the blue and whites thrashed Attercliffe 8-1 before a truly
embarrassing afternoon at Staveley where a Wednesday side, containing
only a sprinkling of senior men, found themselves five goals in arrears at
half-time and suffered a 9-0 thrashing.

The shocking loss was hardly the ideal preparation for the Sheffield Cup
Final meeting with Ecclesfield, but it was perhaps an early example of key

The younger brother of Charles, William Clegg was a pivotal figure in the early years of Wednesday FC.

Arthur Dickinson served Wednesday FC from the 1870s until his untimely death in 1930, working as honorary secretary from 1891 until 1920.

Fred Spiksley – the greatest Wednesday FC footballer of the nineteenth century and one of the best ever produced by England.

Popular 1880s player Harry Winterbottom, believed to be wearing a Sheffield FA strip

Billy Mosforth wearing the strip of the Sheffield FA around 1880. The 'little wonder' was one of the greatest players in the early years of Sheffield football.

G. ULLYETT.
BORN OCT. 21, 1851.

George Ullyet was one of the most famous Yorkshire cricketers of the nineteenth century and played for both sections of the Wednesday Club.

Rear and front of a postcard from 1878, showing the Wednesday FC side that retained the Sheffield Challenge Cup.

LIST OF MATCHES FOR THE SEASON, 1874-5.

DAY.	DATE.		AGAINST.	CLASS OF MATCH.	PLAYED AT.	RSLT.
Saturday	3rd	OCT.	Attercliffe	1st Twelve	Attercliffe	
Saturday	10th		Practice Match		Myrtle road	
Saturday	17th		Fir Vale	1st Twelve	Fir Vale	
Saturday	24th		Crystal Palace, Thurlstone	Mixed Fourteen	Thurlstone	
Saturday	24th		Broomhall	3rd Fourteen	Myrtle road	
Saturday	31st		Heeley	1st Twelve	Heeley	
Saturday	7th	NOV.	London v. Sheffield.		Bramall lane	
Saturday	14th		Exchange Brewery	14 v. Ex. Brewery 1st 14	Myrtle road	
Saturday	21st		Norfolk	2nd Twelve	Norfolk Park	
Saturday	28th		Norfolk	3rd Fourteen	Myrtle road	
Saturday	5th	DEC.	Practice Match		Myrtle road	
Saturday	12th		Heeley	2nd Fourteen	Heeley	
Saturday	19th		Royal Engineers v. Sheffield.		Bramall lane	
Saturday	25th		Broomhall	1st Fourteen	Ecclesall road	
Monday	28th		Broomhall	2nd Fourteen	Ecclesall road	
Saturday	2nd	JANUARY.	Sheffield v. London.		The Oval, London	
Saturday	2nd		Norfolk	2nd Twelve	Myrtle road	
Saturday	9th		Heeley	2nd Fourteen	Myrtle road	
Saturday	16th		Attercliffe	1st Twelve	Myrtle road	
Saturday	23rd		Derwent	1st Twelve	Sheffield	
Saturday	30th		Crystal Palace, Thurlstone	Mixed Fourteen	Thurlstone	
Saturday	30th		Broomhall	3rd Fourteen	Myrtle road	
Saturday	6th	FEB.	Broomhall	1st Twelve	Myrtle road	
Saturday	13th		Exchange Brewery	14 v. Ex. Brewery 1st 14	Rock street	
Saturday	20th		Norfolk	3rd Fourteen	Norfolk Park	
Saturday	27th		Heeley	1st Twelve	Myrtle road	
Saturday	6th	MAR.	Broomhall	2nd Fourteen	Myrtle road	
Saturday	13th		Derwent	1st Twelve	Derby	
Saturday	20th		Fir Vale	1st Twelve	Myrtle road	

Wednesday FC member's ticket from 1874/75, including first, second and third team fixtures.

Wednesday FC – Sheffield Challenge Cup winners 1881. From left to right, back row: W. Fearnehough, H. Hawksley (president), W. Littlehales (secretary), J. Holmes, Anderton (reporter). Middle row: Charles, Hudson, Gregory, C Stratford, Malpass, E. Buttery. Bottom: Bingley, Lang, W. Stacey, Mosforth, H. Newbould.

Photograph of Wednesday Cricket Club, dated around 1870.

Wednesday FC team group from around 1891, now wearing their famous stripes

VIEW OF THE OLD OLIVE GROVE GROUND.

The much-loved first home of Wednesday FC, Olive Grove. The club played there between 1887 and 1899.

Wednesday FC team photograph from the late 1880s. Note the blue and white halves.

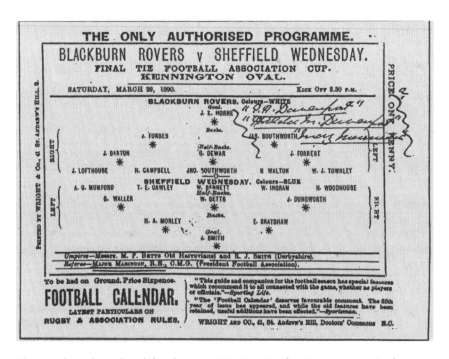

The match card produced for the 1890 FA Cup Final at Kennington Oval, versus Blackburn Rovers.

A sketch of Darnall Cricket Ground, believed to be dated around 1828 – the first home of Sheffield Cricket and of Wednesday Cricket Club.

The Adelphi Hotel, birthplace of Wednesday FC, Sheffield United FC and Yorkshire County Cricket Club.

A plaque on the wall of the Olive Grove Council Depot noting the place of the first real home of Wednesday FC.

Trophy presented by the Wednesday Cricket Club in 1862, at their closing dinner and awards.

The Cromwell Cup – the
second oldest trophy in
world football, won by
Wednesday Football Club
in 1868 and still in the
club's boardroom today.

Winner's medal awarded
to William Clegg after
Wednesday FC won
the inaugural Sheffield
Challenge Cup in 1877.

The original 1871 FA Cup, won
by Wednesday FC in 1896.

Wharncliffe Charity Cup – won
by Wednesday FC in the first
year of competition – 1878/79.
Donated by the Earl of
Wharncliffe and competed for
until the 1980s.

The splendid trophy presented to legendary local cricketer Tom Marsden, in May 1831, by his many friends in the town of Sheffield.

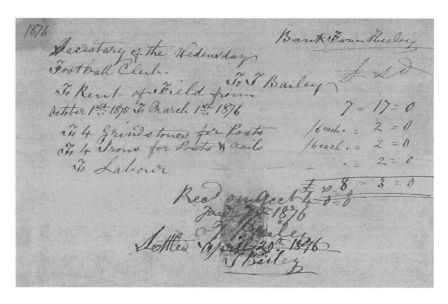

Invoice from 1876 for the rent and provision of goal posts of the club's pitch for the 1875/76 campaign.

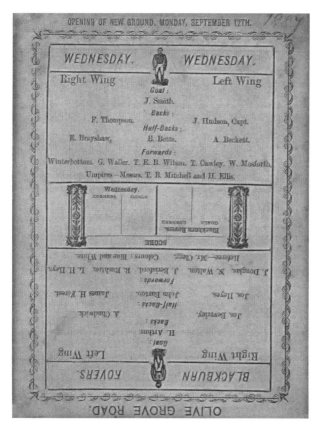

Match Card sold on the day when Wednesday FC opened their new Olive Grove ground with a visit from Blackburn Rovers.

players being 'rested' to ensure Wednesday could field their 'cup side' at the biggest game of the Sheffield football calendar. Whatever the reasons behind the weak side of the previous week, Wednesday were back at full strength and were regarded as hot favourites to carry off the trophy for the third time. Wet weather greeted the teams as they exited the dressing rooms and there was a huge roar, from the estimated 3,000 crowd, when Wednesday captain Gregory kicked off towards Bramall Lane. The pre-match odds would be proven correct as in a totally one-sided final, Wednesday surged to a 8-1 win (the joint biggest victory in the final, shared with Mexborough Athletic in 1934) with the incomparable Gregory grabbing a personal tally of five and Mosforth (2), Bingley completing the rout. At the final whistle the victors were vociferously applauded from the field; Mosforth and Gregory were given a huge ovation by the delighted Wednesday fans.

A week later, Exchange and Wednesday met at the Sheaf House grounds – Bramall Lane having ceased football activities for the season in preparation for cricket – after the respective club secretaries decided to organise a charity game to benefit the medical charities of the town. The game, which effectively replaced the final of the withdrawn Wharncliffe Cup, ended 2-0 to Exchange while the season ended with a fourth trip of the season to the Blackburn area, Rovers gaining some consolation for their FA Cup exit with a 7-3 win. It should also be noted that the game was the first time Wednesday played a fixture in April. Overall the season had been a great success and Easter Monday saw the club's fourteenth annual athletics day, on a sunny but cold day at Bramall Lane. Among the many helpers were the Clegg brothers, former Sheffield FA secretary Pierce-Dix and Francis Butler. The first race – a 2-mile handicap event – went to player Fred Newbould, aided by a 180-yard start. The 440-yard handicap steeplechase proved dramatic as a field full of Wednesday's best players saw the 'little wonder' Mosforth pass Hunter almost on the line to take the glory. The 220-yard handicap race was won by Lang, and it was commented that the sports were again well managed and highly successful – a real tribute to the club's hierarchy.

TOM CAWLEY

Another club legend from the era, Tom Cawley represented Wednesday for over a decade, although he was perhaps more famous for his role in turning Wednesday professional in 1887. He was, however, an outstanding forward; his skill and superb ball control marking him out in an era when 'kick and rush' football was still prevalent. He was born in Sheffield on 2 January 1860 and played the majority of his football with

Wednesday, scoring twenty-two times in thirty-seven FA Cup ties, as well as playing in forty-nine Alliance games. He also appeared in twenty-nine inter-association games for Sheffield and won a multitude of medals in local football in addition to playing in the 1890 FA Cup final. He was also an excellent cricketer and won several medals on the running track. He was deservedly awarded a benefit season in 1890/91 – raising over £182. The fund also brought Mrs Cawley a locket! After retiring in 1892 he coached Wednesday's reserve side and eventually became assistant trainer to Charles Parramore, just before the First World War. His son, also called Tom, played for Wednesday during the conflict. His father lived to the age of seventy-three before passing in Sheffield on 28 January 1933.

The close of the season saw Hudson join the Wednesday committee. The 1881/82 campaign would arguably be the club's most successful of the pre-professional age, with a run to the last four of the FA Cup coupled with success in the Wharncliffe Cup. The long-established Attercliffe versus Wednesday game was now generally recognised as the opening of the football season in Sheffield, and around 500 fans watched the hosts, who included three brothers, face a Wednesday side that was lacking James Lang, who it was believed had left for Derby. However, the visiting side still included several of their 'cup side' plus the Ledger brothers and Rhodes, so it was a surprise for Wednesday to be trailing 3-0 at the interval and lose 4-1, with Gregory opening the club's account for the season. The Sheffield Cup started particularly early and the club's opening home fixture, again with Bramall Lane the preferred venue, came in the first round of the tournament, against the unknown quantity of Eckington Colleries. The visitors ensured any complacency did not creep into the Wednesday team, by taking a shock early lead, but the cup holders recovered strongly to record a 4-1 win. Both Hallam and Wednesday were then poorly represented for a club match at Sandygate before Wednesday were back at Bramall Lane a week later with the Wharncliffe Cup again being the centre of controversy as Heeley met White Star, followed by the blue and whites facing Staveley. The first game was completed without incident, but trouble came to the surface in the second tie after Bingley equalised a first minute strike. The Staveley men immediately appealed to referee William Clegg that Bingley was offside, and when he waved away all appeals eight of the Staveley side walked off the pitch in protest. The crowd made their displeasure known to the visitors and the game was subsequently awarded to Wednesday by the organising committee – Wednesday remained on the pitch until the 90 minutes had elapsed to claim the tie. Seven days later,

Wednesday faced old adversaries Heeley at Bramall Lane in a benefit game for a great servant to Sheffield football, Heeley captain and secretary John Deans. He had primarily been involved with the Heeleyites for eighteen years, also playing the occasional game for Wednesday, but his heart always remained at Meersbrook Park. A crowd of around 1,000 watched Wednesday win 5-1, ensuring the gate receipts greatly increased his benefit pot. It was then FA Cup time, with Wednesday drawn at fellow Sheffield side Providence. The teams met at Quibell's Field near Hyde Park, but the late arrival of the home side meant the match kicked off 15 minutes late. Incredibly, the game was then stopped after 10 minutes and after a recount of the players it was discovered that Providence had twelve men. After the unscheduled arithmetic, the game proved to be a hard-fought encounter, which Wednesday, despite star man Gregory being a passenger after being injured just after half-time, would dominate and progress 2-0, although the ball was only put through the opponents' posts once. The reason came after 60 minutes had been played when an effort on goal from Anthony was handled on the line by a home player and subsequently cleared away. However, a new ruling, which had already come to the club's aid in a Sheffield Cup tie, meant that the referee awarded a goal despite the ball not having breached the goal line. An opening goal from Cawley had put his side on the way to victory, and after four successive away draws in the competition Wednesday experienced a slice of luck when they received a bye in the second round – one of five fortunate clubs, including Aston Villa and Dreadnought. Wednesday were brought back down to earth a week later when they paid a return visit to their FA Cup conquers of the previous season, Darwen, and lost 7-2. The following three matches ended in stalemate, with two of games being against perennial rivals Heeley in the Sheffield Cup, commencing with a thrilling 3-3 draw, which featured two stunning 40-yard goals from Anthony. The Heeleyites led 2-1, their fans clapping, shouting and throwing their hats up into the air when they went ahead, but those two spectacular strikes ensured a replay two weeks later. Sandwiched in-between was a low key 0-0 match at Spital Chesterfield while Wednesday called upon the services of well-known local handicap runner L. McLoughlin for the Heeley replay, the sides drawing 1-1 after Sheel had put Wednesday in front just before the interval. The tie was finally settled at the third attempt with Heeley dumping the holders out of the competition in a game where the second half was played in a 'pea soup' fog and finished in almost total darkness.

HARRY WINTERBOTTOM

In a playing career spanning over twenty years, flying winger Harry Winterbottom represented several clubs in the area, although he was mainly known as a Wednesday player, appearing in the club's first FA Cup tie. Fleet of foot and a fine marksman, Winterbottom created countless goals for others, although he did score 10 in twenty-two FA Cup ties for Wednesday. He also appeared in twenty-eight Alliance League games and put the fear into most full-backs when he came careering down the wing, his not inconsiderable frame also helping. Born in Sheffield on 19 December 1861, Harry was so keen on the game that in 1872 he set up his own club – Suffolk FC – where he acted as captain, treasurer and secretary before joining Wednesday in 1879. He was a vital player as the club rose to become the dominant force in Sheffield and he represented the local FA thirty times. When Wednesday turned professional he remained an amateur – he was a highly skilled cutlery worker – and although he left to play a solitary game at West Bromwich Albion he quickly returned. Injury meant he missed an FA Cup Final appearance, but his service was rewarded with a benefit match a year later. He remained Wednesday 'through and through' and passed away early in 1936, aged seventy-four.

Cup ties dominated the fixture list and the subsequent FA Cup meeting with Staveley – Wednesday finally getting a home draw – would mirror the Heeley match as it required three games to decide the victor. The first tie took place in late December 1881, at Bramall Lane, with a crowd of around 2,000 watching the Derbyshire visitors take the lead only for Rhodes to level and Cawley to put Wednesday ahead 'amid deafening cheers'. However, despite Wednesday being on top, the visitors forced a replay after Marples levelled the score. Before the replay, Bramall Lane was again the venue for a double header in the Wharncliffe Cup semi-finals, with Wednesday versus Lockwood Brothers (including Housley and Tom Buttery) and Heeley versus Attercliffe meeting. On a truly sodden playing surface, Wednesday kicked off first and recorded a convincing 7-2 victory, with four different men netting. It was no surprise that Heeley joined them in the final as the two sides continued to fight for the honour of Sheffield's best club. The opening Saturday of 1882 saw Wednesday again play two games on the same day, with the first choice side travelling to Staveley for the FA Cup replay and a shadow eleven travelling to Lancashire Cup holders Accrington. The latter fixture saw Wednesday, captained by Housley, lose 4-1, although the pitch was described as 'more like a swamp than a football field'. The game in Derbyshire was again a hard-fought encounter, with the sides level at the break before Wednesday went down to ten men after key player Anthony was forced to retire injured mid-way through the second period. The away side gamely hung on though and after an additional 30 minutes of extra time, the teams could still not be separated. Wednesday subsequently won the toss of the coin and nominated Lockwood Brothers' ground – later a home to Sheffield FC – as the venue for the third game; this was played on the following Monday afternoon. The unavailability of the injured Anthony opening the door for Pyebank Club player Stevens, who replaced the experienced attacker and remained in the side for the remainder of Wednesday's cup run. The third match proved a 'bridge too far' for Staveley as Wednesday used their 'home' advantage fully to race away to a 5-1 success, with Cawley, Stevens, Gregory, Cawley again (scoring 'via his noddle') and Fred West completing the rout. However, it is not officially known who actually scored for Wednesday on that day as the two main newspapers in Sheffield at the time – the *Sheffield and Rotherham Independent* and the *Sheffield Evening Telegraph* – recorded totally different scores, with Rhodes credited with 4 goals and Cawley just 1 in the other version of events.

EDWARD BRAYSHAW

Teddy Brayshaw was another outstanding player of the pre-league era, the left-back amassing twenty-one FA Cup ties for Wednesday and thirty games in the Alliance League. Sheffield-born in 1863, he was the son of well-known detective Richard, although his father died in 1867 leaving Teddy to be brought up by his mother, Martha. His football career started at All Saints around 1882 before he appeared for Heeley and then Walkley, being capped by the Sheffield FA. He joined Wednesday around 1883 and became an automatic choice for several seasons, winning his sole cap for England in 1887. He joined the Wednesday committee in 1885 – serving for two seasons – and was part of the 'rebel' group of players who formed Sheffield Rovers to effectively force Wednesday to turn professional. Ironically, he remained amateur throughout his career, working as a carpenter, and missed only four games as Wednesday won the inaugural Alliance League, also appearing in the 1890 FA Cup Final. In January 1889, he took a public house. A series of injuries, which included a broken bone in his left foot, eventually forced his retirement in 1892. Sadly, he also experienced several personal problems and, after ill health meant he could no longer work, could be found in a Sheffield workhouse in 1907 where he tried to commit suicide, cutting his throat with a table knife. Unfortunately, his health deteriorated further and he died, aged only forty-four, in the South Yorkshire Asylum on 20 November 1908. It was a tragic end for an early Wednesday hero.

Immediately following the FA Cup success, Wednesday literally revisited old ground as a small crowd watched a scratch side lose to Exchange in a game played back at their old Myrtle Road home. Wednesday would also play Spital Chesterfield on their old stomping ground at the end of January, losing 4-0, with 'keeper Champion keeping the score down. Prior to that fixture all eyes turned to the FA Cup and Heeley, in the fourth round at Bramall Lane. There was huge interest in the tie – around 4,000 paid for admittance, with the local bookmakers installing Wednesday as slight 5/4 favourites. Early in the game, Wednesday's Malpass hit the ball so hard that it actually burst – play being held up for a while to source a new ball – but it would be Wednesday who exacted their revenge for the Sheffield Cup exit by recording a 3-1 success, with goals from Rhodes, Cawley and Mosforth securing the win. Opponents in the next round were London-based amateur club Upton Park, who were one of the original fifteen entrants in the inaugural season of the FA Cup in 1871.

They were also credited with triggering, unintentionally, the legalisation of professionalism after complaining to the FA in 1884 after being knocked out by Preston North End, who at that point was making payments to their players. The Lancashire club were kicked out of the competition, but the incident brought the issue to the fore. Unfortunately, the southerners had neither a Saturday nor a Monday at liberty, so the fixture took place on a Tuesday afternoon – a date usually avoided by local teams as it was market day in Sheffield. The tie against Upton Park was the first major fixture to be played on that day in Sheffield, the day gradually losing its importance over time. As expected, the game drew a much smaller crowd than normal, but those who did forgo the market were treated to an outstanding display from Wednesday as they rattled in 6 goals without reply to progress to the semi-finals. The visitors kicked off towards Shoreham Street, and were quickly on the back foot, conceding first-half goals to Rhodes and Cawley as the hosts took command. Wednesday duly ran away with the match in the second period, with the third goal, scored by Mosforth, described as 'one of the most magnificent runs ever seen, nearly the whole length of the field, was made by the little wonder, who was totally unsupported, and he did not finish his good exertions until he had put the leather between the Upton 'sticks'. Cawley and Mosforth grabbed the fourth and fifth before the former headed home to complete the first home hat-trick by a Wednesday player in the FA Cup. At the full-time whistle, Mosforth was carried shoulder high from the field and all concerned looked forward to the biggest day so far for Wednesday FC – a cup semi-final clash with Blackburn Rovers.

WILLIAM BETTS

A Wednesday legend of the nineteenth century, Billy Betts played in many of the games that shaped the club, including the opening game at Olive Grove and first matches played in both the Alliance and Football League. He first appeared in Wednesday colours on Boxing Day 1882, but would only play briefly before joining Lockwood Brothers. The club's decision to turn professional saw Betts – known as the 'Old War-horse' – one of the club's first signings, and his no-nonsense and brave centre-back displays endeared him to the Wednesday followers – Billy famously played on in a game with a broken nose! He spent over a decade in Wednesday colours, winning a cap for England in 1889, although he continued to work as a stoker at Neepsend Gas Works and worked full-time before doing battle on the football field. Described as a 'centre half in a thousand', he helped Wednesday become established in the Football League and was rewarded with a benefit game in 1894, retiring a few months later. He did, however, continue to play cricket in the summer months – he was a player of considerable ability – and was still donning the whites into his mid-forties. Later in life he worked as a groundsman at Wednesday, and, after assisting the 'A' team, was appointed assistant trainer in 1922. He eventually retired, passing away on 8 August 1941, although his grandson, Dennis Woodhead, kept the family connection alive.

Before the big day, Heeley and Wednesday would meet for the sixth and seventh time in the season, commencing with a 3-3 score in a club game. Strangely, Wednesday did not play another game in the month of February and actually met Heeley again, in the final of the Wharncliffe Cup, on the Saturday before the FA Cup semi-final – the last four clash being almost squeezed into the schedule on a Monday afternoon, which was a far cry from the luxuries afforded to the modern-day competition. The final of the Charity Cup was due to take place a week later, but this clashed with the England versus Scotland international so was brought forward seven days. A healthy crowd (including a sprinkling of the 'fairer sex') watched the proceedings, which commenced when Hunter kicked off for Heeley.

Wednesday's opponents also included the up-and-coming Billy Betts in their ranks, and the blue and whites suffered the early blow of losing Mosforth to injury. Thankfully, he returned to the fold after 10 minutes in the dressing rooms. Goals just before half-time from Gregory and Cawley put the favourites in command. Wednesday attacker Cawley would go on to complete a hat-trick, in a 5-0 success, as his side emphatically proved who the champion club of Sheffield was. Of course, Wednesday were also challenging strongly for recognition on a countrywide basis, with an appearance in the last four of the FA Cup contributing significantly to this aim. The big game was fixed for the St John's Club ground in Huddersfield – a venue more commonly called the Fartown Ground, home to Huddersfield RLC from 1878–1992. The game was the only association football match ever played at the ground and it caused immense interest both locally and nationally; trains ran from various parts of the country to see if Wednesday could upset 2-1 favourites Rovers. A special train from Sheffield, run by Messers Drake & Dawson, carried the team and 900 other excursionists, although its late arrival meant the teams kicked off later than advertised at 3.20 p.m. The Lancastrians won the toss and Lang, seemingly back in Sheffield and recalled to the side, kicked off for the Yorkshiremen, kicking up a hill against both sun and wind. The tie proved to be as tight as expected, and despite some 'capital play', and both sides having goals disallowed, it remained 0-0 deep into the second half. Shouts of 'well played Sheffield' could be heard from the sidelines from a huge crowd, which generated receipts of £142, 6s and 5d. Just before the end it was announced that an extra 30 minutes would be played if the game finished level, but Wednesday declined to agree so the match went to a replay nine days later in Manchester. It later transpired that during the tie, several Wednesday players believed that the ball had gone through the Blackburn posts, but captain Lang, who usually appealed for everything, did not on this occasion claim a goal to the referee. The official later admitted that he would have awarded the point if he had done so – a story of what might have been! The venue for the second game, known as the Whalley Range or Fallowfield Ground, actually hosted the 1893 FA Cup Final and was the scene of several cup wins by the fledgling Newton Heath (Manchester United) in the nineteenth century.

GEORGE CROPPER

Born around 1849, George Cropper joined the club's committee in 1882 and served for four years before he was appointed joint club secretary, with Jack Hudson. He remained in the role for two seasons, arranging the club's athletics days, before resigning in 1888. He had briefly played as a goalkeeper in his younger days – playing against Wednesday for Exchange in October 1880 – but was mainly utilised in administrative roles, also serving on the committee of the Sheffield FA in the 1880s. He married wife Anne in 1873 and was father to two children, living on West Street in Sheffield. He followed in his father's footsteps, working as a gas fitter/ bell hanger.

Special trains again ferried eager fans to the tie, with an estimated attendance of around 10,000 at the fixture, which would provide the first ever 'provincial' club to appear in a FA Cup Final. The match was level at the break, after an own goal put Wednesday ahead, but the wide pitch proved an advantage for Rovers who were blessed with fast wing men and better all round fitness. They put Wednesday under enormous pressure in the second half, and with star man Mosforth visibly tiring Rovers effectively killed off the tie after scoring twice in a 5-minute spell and completing a 5-1 win, clinching a meeting with Old Etonians. The defeat was somewhat harsh on a plucky Wednesday side, but the club's name was now well renowned around the country thanks to two eye-catching runs in the 'blue ribbon' event of the national football calendar. Despite the increasing popularity of football, the club's sports day was still well attended, and the fifteenth edition of the Sheffield Wednesday Cricket and Football Club athletics day saw the crowds entertained by the Dore brass band. Winners on the day included Hudson (120-yard race) and Mosforth (440-yard handicap steeplechase). Committeemen Donovan and Cawthron collected over £3 for the Blue Coat boys – students of a local charity school – with some fifty or sixty lads running once around the track before the 'bounty' was shared out between them.

Another New Ground, the Wednesday Club Splits in Two and a Fall from Grace

The summer's AGM saw Henry Ledger join the committee while other newcomers included Henry Wilkinson and George Cropper. The club's successes of the early 1880s also meant an increasing workload for secretary Littlehales. His burden was eased when Herbert Muscroft moved into the newly created role of assistant secretary. The new season opened with Wednesday's first ever game in the month of September – a sign of the growing fixture list – although the opponents were unchanged with Attercliffe playing host. Wednesday included the Newbould brothers Fred and Herbert, and the team scored two quick goals, eventually winning 3-1. The second Saturday of the new campaign took Wednesday to Darwen, but they travelled with virtually a scratch side after the Sheffield FA called up most of their best players. A 6-1 defeat followed before Mosforth was on the scoresheet in a 2-2 draw with Spital Chesterfield at Bramall Lane. The club then faced a quartet of away fixtures, commencing with a first meeting with Aston Villa at their old Perry Bar ground. The visit of the well-known Wednesday club created great interest in Birmingham, but the visitors, lacking key men, found themselves 4-1 in arrears at the interval after the home side proved stronger than expected. Wednesday – who were called the 'Blades' for the first time in a match report – had goalkeeper Ledger to thank for keeping the score down, limiting the defeat to a mere 6-1. It was then time for the Sheffield Cup and a trip for Wednesday into the unknown as the draw sent them to Leeds-based minnows Oulton. Wednesday would subsequently score an incredible 27 goals in their next three fixtures, commencing with an 8-0 stroll in Leeds and ending with a 7-0 Wharncliffe Cup win against Walkley. In between those fixtures, Wednesday welcomed Lincolnshire Cup holders Spilsby to Bramall Lane, in the first round of the FA Cup, and set a new club record by registering an astonishing 12-2 success. Only four players were on the scoresheet that day, with Gregory becoming the first player to score 5 goals for Wednesday in a senior game while Cawley and Herbert Newbould both helped themselves to hat-tricks.

Incidentally, in the same period the club's reserve side played their first game in the newly introduced Sheffield FA Minor Cup competition and promptly won 10-1 at Walkley reserves. However, that resounding win was somewhat negated in the next round when they lost 10-0 at home to Lockwood Brothers reserves! It was reported that the home fans were on 'tip toes of excitement' during the subsequent 2-1 defeat at Blackburn Rovers, although Wednesday considered themselves unlucky with both of the home goals hotly disputed.

CARL AND WALPOLE HILLER

The Hiller brothers were both highly educated 'gentleman' players of the 1880s, remaining amateur throughout their careers. Older brother Carl was born in 1866 and traded for many years from his Barkers Pool Pork Butchers shop while playing mainly for Heeley and the occasional game for Wednesday. He appeared in five FA Cup games for Wednesday, scoring once, and was still a teenager when he made his cup debut. Although married to Isabella in 1888, the pair separated in 1899 and in April 1911 she was found dead after falling while intoxicated. His brother Walpole, born 17 August 1867, was educated at Trinity College, Harrogate, and after attending Wesley College in Sheffield he went into the law profession, eventually qualifying as a solicitor in 1890. He was regarded as one of Sheffield's finest all round sportsman, excelling at football, cricket, cycling and swimming. Walpole was a real character and was a lover of the open air – he could often been seen striding along in a sports jacket, a tweed sports hat and a flowing black cravat. He was a popular figure in sporting and law circles and, unlike his brother, played most of his football in Wednesday colours. He appeared in only one FA Cup tie for Wednesday, in January 1885, and was also a keen cricketer who was said to often record the 'hat-trick' as a bowler – he once took seven consecutive wickets while playing for Wesley College in 1883. He played briefly in the Alliance League for Wednesday before a dose of influenza curtailed his football activities. He was, however, more famous for his swimming feats, taking 5 hours and 44 minutes to swim from London to Gravesend in 1907, and assisting in several cross channel swims – he was quoted as saying 'I have been a human fish for ten years'. He died suddenly after collapsing on a tramcar and was DOA at hospital on 24 November 1927, aged sixty. He left a widow and two sons, one of whom continued to run the Nether Edge family law firm.

A week later, another new era in the club's history began with the first home game played at Hunter's Bar after Wednesday left Sheaf House to move to the fringes of the town centre. However, despite another change of home, Bramall Lane continued to be the club's first choice for all major cup ties and Hunter's Bar, like its predecessor Sheaf House, would be used in the main just for minor and reserve games. The club's new home was believed to have been just off modern-day Ecclesall Road, near the Hunter's Bar roundabout. The ground, often referred to as Robert's Farm or Rustling's Farm, was situated on farmland just off the main road – Rustlings Road runs around the southern side of Endcliffe Park. It was later described as 'near to the bathing dam in Endcliffe Park' and common opinion suggests the actual pitch was situated where the modern day Hallamshire Tennis Club stands.

The first game, in November 1882, saw Thurlstone visit Sheffield although for a variety of reasons the match did not start until 4.00 p.m., at which point both sides agreed to play two halves of just 20 minutes. Despite Wednesday being considerably weakened for the abridged friendly, again due to Sheffield FA call ups, a comfortable 5-0 win was recorded against the 'Thurlstonites', with H. Cawthorne scoring the first goal at Hunter's Bar after 2 minutes. Wednesday remained near Ecclesall Road for their next fixture, visiting Lockwood Brothers in the next round of the FA Cup. An overnight frost meant the playing surface was hard and slippy, but with fans lining the pitch, Wednesday coped better with the conditions, after winning the toss and kicking towards Ecclesall Road. The partnership of Anthony and Mosforth quickly brought an opening goal for the former, while the latter later scored a brilliant individual goal as Wednesday recorded a comprehensive 6-0 win to progress. Wednesday would not play again until after Christmas Day when a visit to the Britannia Grounds, Brigg, commenced a packed holiday programme. The visit to Brigg certainly fell into the category of 'missionary' games as Wednesday showed greater 'speed, science and stamina', and virtually the club's 'cup side' won 5-0 in a game where 'keeper Ledger hardly touched the ball. The return game with Thurlstone ended with 6 goals shared before it was Sheffield Cup quarter-final time, against Pyebank at Bramall Lane.

Despite a heavy fall of snow, the cup tie still went ahead with Wednesday squeezing through 3-2, a 'pile-driver' from Gregory proving decisive. New addition Billy Betts made an immediate debut when Wednesday travelled to Nottingham Forest in the next round of the 'English Cup'. The away side also had to make an enforced change when the hosts' objection to Malpass – they claimed he had been paid to play in a match earlier in the season – was upheld and Wednesday drafted in Walkley player Willis Bentley. The fixture would be dogged by appeals and counter appeals as the new vogue of protesting, usually about the ineligibility of an opposition player, became an unwelcome feature of the competition. The tie finished 2-2 – Gregory and Redcar player William Harrison for Wednesday – and before the replay Forest captain Sam Widdowson went to extraordinary lengths in an attempt to launch another appeal. He actually travelled to Sheffield to go through the Wednesday minute books and even plastered posters around the town offering a £20 reward for any evidence that any players were not bona-fide members of Wednesday. His sterling efforts were unrewarded and the replay went ahead on a mud splattered Bramall Lane pitch, which looked like a 'ploughed field' – Forest played 'under protest' due to the quality of the surface. A crowd of 3,000 attended the fixture and saw Wednesday establish a 3-0 interval lead thanks to goals from Harrison (a strike that 'brought the house down'), Mosforth (one of his trademark individual efforts) and Harrison again. The Foresters fought back in the second period, but despite pulling 2 goals back it was Wednesday who maintained their proud record of reaching the fourth round of the tournament for the third consecutive season. Incidentally, after losing, Forest protested again, this time about the ineligibility of players, but the FA committee eventually dismissed the claims and officially censured them.

WILLIS BENTLEY

Willis Bentley was a utility player who appeared in several positions for Wednesday, including half-back, full-back and inside forward. Born in Sheffield in 1862, Bentley played for Exchange and Walkley before spending just over two years in Wednesday colours, playing primarily at half-back. His senior debut came in a FA Cup tie at Nottingham Forest, and he helped Wednesday to lift the Wharncliffe Cup in the same year. His final appearance came in a friendly against Derby County, in November 1885, before spending four years with Owlerton. He also briefly appeared for the fledgling Sheffield United before winning both the Midland League and Lincolnshire Cup with Gainsborough Trinity in the 1890s. His football career came to a close after a spell at Stockport County, although he later worked alongside ex-Wednesday man Betts, around the turn of the century, in coaching and developing Owlerton-based side Channing Rovers. Bentley was also a keen cricketer, playing for Owlerton, Neepsend Gas Works and Wadsley Asylum. He worked at the latter for several years as a tutor/warder, teaching both football and cricket to the patients, and was also employed as both a steel tilter and gas stoker at various times in his life. Bentley married wife Hannah in 1887 with whom he had five children, although only one survived – a sad but not uncommon occurrence in Victorian life. Bentley himself died suddenly of pneumonia, aged around fifty-four, on 2 September 1916.

Thoughts then briefly turned away from the excitement of the FA Cup with Wednesday, who included cricketer George Ulyett in goal, losing to Walsall Town at the Chuckery Grounds. Local rivals Walkley were then beaten in the first round of the Wharncliffe Cup before the FA Cup pitched another Nottingham side against Wednesday, with County travelling to Sheffield. Such was the interest in the tie that a record crowd approaching 10,000 was anticipated at Bramall Lane, but heavy rain on the day severely reduced the attendance with around only 2,000 braving the inclement conditions. Wednesday gave cup debuts to both Pyebank player George Bowns and goalie Ulyett as they looked to complete a Nottingham 'double' and progress to the last eight. Unfortunately, the blue and whites never looked likely to overcome a County side that actually sent a telegram before the game to say they could not fulfil the tie as they couldn't raise a team. They did, however, put in an appearance and in pouring rain led 3-1 at the break - Bentley for Wednesday – before a second-half strike ended dreams of glory. It was therefore back to local issues, with Wharncliffe and Sheffield Cup semi-finals both against fierce rivals Attercliffe. The two ties were preceded by a challenge match at Hunter's Bar against Darwen. Despite Wednesday missing five key players – all representing the Sheffield FA in Glasgow – they led 2-0 before having to settle for parity after a 2-2 draw.

HENRY HALL LEDGER

Goalkeeper Henry Ledger followed in the footsteps of the Stacey brothers as one of the club's early custodians. Born in 1856, Henry started his career at Hallam, playing both football and cricket. When he was a teenager he also played the summer game with the likes of Heeley and St Stephens. His Wednesday career started when he appeared between the sticks in a November 1880 friendly against Heeley, and made his senior debut in the club's second FA Cup tie at Turton in 1881. Henry would play in thirteen of Wednesday's first sixteen ties in the competition and also won both the Sheffield Cup and Wharncliffe Cup while wearing the blue and white. He also represented the Sheffield FA, but eventually lost his place to George Ulyett during the 1882/83 campaign and seemingly dropped out of football altogether.

The double header for the semi-finals of the Charity Cup were played at the Newhall Grounds as opposed to the usual Bramall Lane setting, and on a fine sunny day Pyebank faced Staveley and Wednesday met Attercliffe. The vast majority parted with their hard-earned money to see the clash of the two Sheffield sides. It looked like Attercliffe had taken the lead when the ball nestled in the net from a long throw in. However, the goal was disallowed as no other player had touched the ball and Wednesday overcome that early scare to record a 4-2 victory and maintain their record of having reached every final since the competition was introduced. A fortnight later the two sides reconvened, at Bramall Lane this time, to fight for a place in the final of the prestigious Sheffield Cup, but Wednesday could only field a relatively weak side and looked unlikely to repeat the earlier victory. Wednesday did though go into the break ahead, a splendid left foot shot from Gregory, and looked set to spring a surprise win when Herbert Newbould doubled their advantage in the second period. However, the game went into extra time and Wednesday trailed 3-2 as the tie entered its final minute, only for the two earlier scorers to combine and Gregory to poach a dramatic leveller. The combatants met again on Easter Saturday, and it was Wednesday who went through at the second attempt, an error from goalkeeper Jackson gifting them an early goal before Gregory charged the custodian over the line, along with the ball, to seal a 2-0 success and yet another cup final appearance for the town's most successful and best supported club. For the first time since Wednesday started their athletics days, the sixteenth instalment of the popular event actually fell within the football season in 1883, taking place on Easter Monday.

The day's activities commenced at 1.30 p.m., with the usual large number of Wednesday officials on hand, including Holmes, Hawksley and the Fearnehough brothers, to ensure the well attended annual event was again run successfully. Included in the fourteen-strong programme was a 120-yard handicap flat race while the 1-mile bicycle race saw one-legged man W.B. Fountain win his first heat, much to the delight of crowd, before fading in the final to finish third. Indomitable crowd favourite Mosforth again delighted his admirers by surging through the field in the 440-yard steeplechase – it was thought the 'little wonder' had been unfairly handicapped – to just beat fellow Wednesday footballer Walter Edmund Jaques by just over a yard. The first three places in the 150-yard hurdle race were all taken by football players – Hudson, Bowns and Mosforth. The sports ended promptly at 6.00 p.m. after Wednesday had maintained their reputation for offering the best athletics day in the region. Probably due to Wednesday's involvement in the FA Cup and several replays in the local cup competitions that the final of the Sheffield Cup was actually played in midweek, just three days after the semi-final. Opponents for 6-4 favourites Wednesday were works side Lockwood Brothers, who had now become a force on the local scene. They did indeed prove tough opponents, and it needed goals from Gregory and Mosforth to earn a second bite of the cherry – extra time not being played after one of the team captains refused the option. Wednesday were back at

Bramall Lane on the following Saturday, for the final of the Charity Cup, with Pyebank hoping to wrestle the trophy from the holders. Former Wednesday man Tom Buttery was drafted into the opponents' ranks while Ulyett was again between the sticks for the blue and whites. However, on a glorious spring afternoon, the final proved decidedly one-sided, although Pyebank did keep Wednesday out until 55 minutes had elapsed when the ball was 'put through' after an almighty scrimmage in front of the posts, the score being met with 'hearty applause' from Wednesday fans. The goal opened the proverbial floodgates and Wednesday would breach their opponents' goal line on three more occasions to wrap up a comfortable success and retain the trophy. Usually the season would end in late March, but it was a sign of the times, and the ever increasing popularity of football, that Wednesday still had three more fixtures plus a benefit game for popular captain Gregory. The replay of the Sheffield Cup Final was first with the Buttery brothers again in opposition. This time though Wednesday took a firm grip with Fred Newbould and Mosforth putting them 2-0 ahead in front of around 5,000 people. The works side did pull a goal back but Wednesday held on to clinch the Sheffield 'double' of Challenge and Charity cups.

ALFRED HOLMES

Sheffield born in 1849, Alfred was a successful businessman who assisted Wednesday for many years behind the scenes. A partner in Tysack and Holmes, rule and measure manufacturers on Cavendish Street, Alfred joined the club's committee in 1883 and became vice president in 1887, serving in that role, and that of treasurer, when Wednesday were elevated into the Football League. He was described as a whole-hearted supporter of the team, retiring and unobtrusive, and his success in business meant he lived in the salubrious surrounds of a country house at Hodsock Park near Worksop with his family and four servants. Unfortunately, his story has a sad ending as travelling home one evening his horses were disturbed and his carriage collided with his entrance gate, throwing Alfred and his wife out. His spouse survived with cuts and bruises, but Alfred was kicked in the face by a frightened horse and almost killed on site. He briefly recovered but eventually passed away at his home, aged fifty-three, on 2 June 1902.

Two days later, Bramall Lane hosted a benefit game for Gregory with an over twenty-fives side facing an under twenty-fives side, with his popularity shown as Blackburn Olympic players Hunter and Wilson travelled from Lancashire and a healthy crowd watched as the older players beat the young 'uns. A low-key defeat at Sheffield-based side Surrey followed – Wednesday fielding only Anthony with any significant first team experience – before the season came to a close on 16 April at home to Blackburn Rovers. The match had been postponed in late March due to the semi-final of the Sheffield Cup, and as Hunter's Bar and Bramall Lane were both unavailable, Wednesday borrowed Attercliffe's Newhall Grounds. It was Malpass who kicked off, towards Grimesthorpe, but a keenly fought game would end in the visitors' favour to conclude yet another successful season. After the great triumphs of the early 1880s, Wednesday seemed destined to remain the most popular and successful side in Sheffield, but fortunes would turn significantly in the four years that followed and by the spring of 1887 even their very existence seemed in doubt. However, at the club's AGM in the summer of 1883 the mood was, unsurprisingly, upbeat, as several changes were made behind the scenes. The new secretary was James Hoyland, with previous incumbent Littlehales appointed to the new role of treasurer. New onto the committee were Alfred Holmes, Herbert Newbould, Sydney Stratford (rejoining) and Charles Vessey; Malpass stepped down. The new campaign opened, for what proved the final time, at Attercliffe, who were now playing at the Old Forge Ground.

A much changed Wednesday side – including new goalkeeper Fred Bye, William Moss, Jaques and Thomas Hardman – adapted well to a poor pitch to win 6-1. A week later the season was opened at Hunter's Bar with success over Rotherham. A revisit to the factory club of Spital Chesterfield was next on the agenda, with the meeting uniquely bringing together the holders of Sheffield FA and Hallamshire Association cups. Despite that fact, only a poor crowd attended (Spital would soon become defunct) to watch Wednesday, including new full-back Jack Jeeves, record a third consecutive victory, continuing an excellent start to the season. There was then an early start in the club's defence of the Sheffield Cup with a long trip to Redcar for the opening tie in the tournament. As expected, Wednesday were comfortable winners on the north-east coast, with hat-tricks from Bentley and Cawley helping the visitors to a 7-1 success, watched by a bumper 3,000-strong crowd. The biggest test of Wednesday's 100 per cent start to the season came a fortnight later when Blackburn Rovers visited Bramall Lane. When Wednesday won an early throw in, fans would have seen a new ruling – it was now law to throw the ball directly over the thrower's head into play. Goalie Ulyett kept a clean sheet as his side recorded a 2-0 success. A sixth consecutive victory was recorded in a first meeting with Deepcar, facing the village side in a field opposite the Blue Ball Inn, Wharncliffe Side. A strong Wednesday side won comfortably, watched by several hundred spectators, although the game proved bittersweet for Ulyett as an injury he received would bring his football career to a premature end.

ARTHUR JOSHUA DICKINSON

Locally born Arthur Dickinson was the club's first great administrator, having joined around 1876. He was a constant behind the scenes, and in 1887 was appointed financial secretary, stepping up to full honorary secretary in 1891. Despite Wednesday turning professional and joining the Football League, Arthur remained employed full-time as a salesman for a Sheffield cutlery firm, and was the only honorary secretary in the league. His remit was far reaching, from scouting players, overseeing the moves to Olive Grove and Owlerton, dealing with the day-to-day financial matters and also having a say in team selection – it was said that during the club's Olive Grove days Arthur would take the gate receipts home and stash them under his bed, waiting for the bank to open on Monday. He was a man with a retiring nature, who loved the country life and cycling, but his first love and passion was Wednesday and he'd serve until just after the First World War, resigning on 18 May 1920. A man not prone to small talk, who took praise and blame with equal equanimity, Arthur continued to help the club and was attending a Football League management committee meeting in London when he collapsed, dying instantly, on 5 November 1930. He was seventy-nine at the time of his passing and left an impression on club history that cannot be underestimated.

The next game was a benefit match for Heeley player Martin, with Wednesday's team including Bye in goal in place of the stricken Ulyett. The club's great start to the season finally ended at the hands of their fierce rivals, Heeley going ahead before going down to ten men during the first half when the beneficiary was forced to retire injured. They made it 2-0 soon after and there was no further scoring as an out of sorts Wednesday went down to a disappointing defeat. A draw followed at Derby Midland where a Wednesday side ravaged by illness included former Walkley player Teddy Brayshaw in their ranks for the first time. Three days later, on 13 November 1883, the club called an extraordinary general meeting of its members at the Adelphi Hotel, where president Hawksley proposed that 'the cricket and football clubs be separated financially'. In the early years of the football club, the cricketers had provided financial assistance, but as Wednesday FC started to outgrow their parent it was commented, admittedly in good humour, that the football club earned all the money and the cricket club spent it.

The motion was carried unanimously and Holmes and Sydney Stratford, representing the football and cricket sections respectively, agreed that the football club would settle the cricket club's present liabilities. It was also proposed that as many subscriptions would be paid to the cricket club as possible before 31 January 1884, at which point the Wednesday FC treasurer would pay the balance owing – this resolution was also carried. From that day forward the financial side of the club split into two, although, for the time being, Wednesday was still a unified force, jointly running the annual sports day while the vast majority of the administration roles were held by a single individual such as president Hawksley. After the historic meeting, Wednesday were without a game until the opening day of December when they travelled to Chesterfield's Recreation Ground for a FA Cup first round tie against Staveley. The game had been switched by the Sheffield FA following an outbreak of what the press called 'foot and mouth disease', alluding to Staveley's crude tackling and foul-mouthed language! Wednesday had already been installed as one of the favourites for the competition, and they handed 'English Cup' debuts to Carl Hiller, Jack Jeeves and 'keeper Lance Morley, but any hopes that losing ground advantage would hamper Staveley were quickly dashed as they raced into a 3-0 lead, leaving Wednesday shell-shocked.

Despite Winterbottom pulling a goal back, Wednesday could do no more and duly exited the tournament. After such a great start to the season, the whole campaign virtually caved in just over 48 hours later as Lockwood Brothers dumped Wednesday out of the Sheffield Cup. The Bramall Lane meeting started brightly enough when a brilliant solo effort from Mosforth put the holders in front, but Wednesday could not hold on and conceded twice to slip out of the competition at the second round stage – post-match rumours abounded that Wednesday were set to protest against the winners, but nothing was forthcoming as the club reeled from two damaging results. A heavy defeat to Bolton club Astley Bridge, at Hunter's Bar, did little to lift fans' spirits before Wednesday experienced a public relations disaster for the meeting with Darwen after increasing the admission costs to 6d. Fans did not take kindly to the price hike and the fixture was boycotted with only around 100 paying for admission. Those that did attend were all drenched at the final whistle (many had left well before the conclusion) as it rained heavily throughout .Wednesday included new goalkeeper Jim Smith, and a goal from Herbert Newbould secured a first win for almost seven weeks. Not for the first time in the season Wednesday were poorly represented for the Christmas Eve meeting with Walsall Town, fielding several virtual unknowns. The inclusion of so many new faces badly disrupted the team pattern and Wednesday lost 3-1 before both parties were entertained at the Star Hotel, High Street.

The constant unavailability of the club's better players was a pattern throughout the season – exits in the two main cup competitions certainly not helping – and the final game of the year exemplified this as Wednesday sent virtually a reserve side to Darwen, losing a decidedly one-sided game 5-2 – a repeat of the FA Cup result almost three years earlier.

GEORGE WILSON

George Wilson was born in Swinton but made his name as a 'thunderous centre forward' for Blackburn Olympic in the early 1880s – winning the FA Cup with the Lancashire side in 1883. During his time at Olympic, the team were training at Blackpool and George, along with teammate Hunter, broke a club curfew and received the 'silent treatment' on the following morning from the other players. However, the mischievous pair filled all the team's pipes with cayenne pepper and the room cleared instantly when the players lit up. Born around 1858, George worked as a glass blower and appeared occasionally for Wednesday FC at full-back including a 7-2 loss at Darwen in 1881, before playing two FA Cup games for the club in the 1884/85 season. He became one of the first professional players at Preston North End before returning home to help Mexborough lift the Sheffield Cup in 1886, playing at centre forward in a win over Heeley.

Wednesday were pleased to see the back of 1883 – a year that had started so brightly but ended so poorly. Unfortunately, the dawn of 1884 did not see an end to the club's woes as 'good old Wednesday' suffered another shock defeat, losing 3-1 to Park Grange (formerly Providence) in the first round of the Wharncliffe Cup. Even the local press, not usually one to comment on such matters, noted that it was 'another of the numerous reverses suffered by the old club'. A heavy defeat at Bolton Wanderers followed before Wednesday returned home to face Heeley at Bramall Lane. The Heeleyites drafted in several men from Lockwood Brothers and Wednesday were seemingly in the rare position of being underdogs as the crown of Sheffield's top side seemed to be slipping. Wednesday were again 'weakly represented', but it was the recruitment of Frank Sugg – who later became a first class cricket umpire – that proved inspirational as the newcomer grabbed 4 goals in a morale boosting 6-3 win, finally giving Wednesdayites something to cheer about.

Any hopes of a revival were quickly dashed on the following Saturday when Wednesbury Town romped to a comprehensive 4-0 win. The defeat must have weighted heavily on the mind of Wednesdayites as their side fielded one of their strongest elevens of the whole campaign, featuring the likes of Edwin Buttery, Gregory, Chas Stratford, Malpass, Mosforth and Cawley. The final game of three consecutive Bramall Lane fixtures saw Notts County visit with Wednesday looking to gain some revenge for the previous season's FA Cup defeat. The game finished goal-less after being played in pouring rain throughout, the pitch being described as a 'perfect puddle', with both players and fans just glad for full-time so they could get home and dry out.

FREDERICK BYE

Frederick Bye was a Sheffield-born goalkeeper who appeared for Wednesday during the mid-1880s. Fred first played for Meersbrook Rangers and Milton Works while he appeared in a representative game for the Sheffield FA as a centre forward. He was an active member of Wednesday in the late 1880s and helped to organise benefits for various players including Dungworth, eventually joining the club committee in 1891. After his playing days ended, Fred became a well-known Football League referee, officiating in the top division and taking charge of a Scotland versus Ireland international. Away from football, he was a keen cyclist and was a member of the Sharrow Cycling Club. He was also heavily involved in athletics, serving in an administrative role for Sheffield United Harriers and Athletics Club. He was a great supporter of all sport and was presented with a silver flower bowl in 1910 for his services, and later served as honorary secretary of the Sheffield Union of Golf Clubs. He was the headmaster of St Mary National School in Sheffield, and was hailed a hero in October 1904 when at the Sheffield school's swimming gala he dived into the pool fully clothed to rescue a drowning pupil. He passed away aged eighty-two in North Yorkshire late in 1948.

Despite Wednesday's unconvincing form, they could still call upon several of Sheffield's best players. This backfired against the club somewhat for the next game when most were called up by the Sheffield FA. The challenge match, against new opponents Derby Midland, was also switched to Lockwood Brothers' Ecclesall Road ground, with both Hunter's Bar and Bramall Lane unavailable. The game would, however, provide a 'shot in the arm' for the club's ailing season as Wednesday crushed their Derbyshire opponents 8-1, although the comprehensive win was aided when injuries saw the visitors reduced to nine men. The next match was at the same venue, but this time Wednesday were the away side as they faced Lockwood Brothers in a benefit game for former player Tom Buttery. Around 800 attended the mid-week game and Wednesday supporters were delighted as their side won 5-2. A few days later, Nottingham Forest and Wednesday met at the Parkside Ground – Forest's home from 1882–85 – with a Winterbottom brace securing another away success. After a stalemate with Lockwood Brothers, the problems of early season re-emerged for the game at Wednesbury Town when Wednesday arrived a player short. A substitute was recruited from the crowd and a superb second-half display earned a 2-0 win to extend the unbeaten run to six games. Wednesday wrapped up the season with away games at Walsall Town and against FA Cup winners Blackburn Rovers. For the game in the West Midlands, Wednesday were again understrength, fielding nothing like the pre-advertised side. They also arrived late, the match not kicking off until almost 5.00 p.m.

Defeat followed while in Lancashire, Wednesday took an early lead but eventually lost 3-1– the match report of the game mentioned that Winterbottom had a great chance, but the home defenders put him 'hors de combat' – a French term which effectively meant he was crowded out. It was also a sign of the expanding fixture list of many football clubs that for a second season running the club's athletics day fell inside the football season, taking place as usual on Easter Monday. Poor weather saw only a small smattering of spectators inside the ground at the 1.00 p.m. start, but as the sun broke from behind the clouds the attendance increased exponentially in line with the rise in temperature, although the figures did not reach the heights of 1883. Early winners included Hudson (300-yard handicap flat race) and Dungworth, who won both the 1-mile handicap and the 700-yard steeplechase. The ever popular Mosforth failed to record a fourth consecutive win in the 440-yard handicap steeplechase after pulling up near the finish line, although the 'little wonder' did not leave without a trophy, winning the 150-yard hurdles race. Unfortunately, mid-afternoon saw the heavy rain return and by the time the 'consolation scramble' had brought the proceedings to a close, officials, spectators and competitors were happy to head for shelter.

LANCELOT ARTHUR MORLEY

Although Lance Morley made a handful of appearances for Wednesday FC, including a FA Cup tie in 1883, the goalkeeper was much better known for his incredible service to the cricket club, which he joined in the mid-1870s and officially wound up in 1924. Born in Worksop in 1858, Morley joined the club's committee in 1878 and was still a serving member and player when he penned a history of the cricket club, published in the *Sheffield Daily Telegraph* in 1896. A year earlier he had taken six Dronfield wickets for only 24 runs while appearing for Wednesday. Away from sport he worked as a relieving officer in Sheffield – an individual who worked for the guardians of the poor, receiving and processing relief applications and reporting on individual circumstances. Lance sadly lost his wife days after she gave birth to his daughter and remained a widower until he passed away in 1935.

At the club's AGM, officials were at pains to point out that Wednesday had beaten the FA Cup winners in the previous season, but it had not been a good campaign for those who sported blue and white favours with twelve wins and eleven defeats from twenty-six first team games. The second team also played on seventeen occasions, but it was perhaps symptomatic of the club's troubles that an eye-watering seventy-three different individuals appeared in those games. New to the committee were Arthur Dickinson and Winterbottom, although Francis Butler resigned his post.

Professional or Not? That is the Question

There was no doubt that the 1883/84 season had been the worst for Wednesday since the town embraced cup football in the late 1870s, but a new campaign brings new hope and the club were proud to announce that they had secured the patronage of several gentlemen, including the Right Honourable Earl of Wharncliffe (whose name adorned the town's Charity Cup) and Sir Frederick Mappin (father of Sheffield University, MP, industrialist and philanthropist), and challenge matches had been arranged with several high-profile clubs. For the first time since 1871, the new season did not open with a game at Attercliffe, Wednesday instead fielding two sides – one at Aston Villa and the other at Hunter's Bar, against Spital Chesterfield. The new campaign started with two wins with the 'shadow' team including Yorkshire CCC player John Wesley Parton. A week later, Wednesday lost narrowly at Bolton Wanderers' Pikes Lane Ground, but the score did not tell the whole story of the game as home goalie Hay spent the match leaning against his goalpost as Wanderers laid siege to the away goal. A win over Mexborough followed – the Hiller brothers appearing for Wednesday – before a meeting with Hallam in what was considered the outstanding tie in the first round of the Sheffield Cup. The game not only showed the humour of Sheffield favourite Billy Mosforth but also one of the major problems suffered by clubs in what was still, in Sheffield anyway, a totally amateur sport. A few weeks before the cup tie, Wesley College were hammered 26-0 after virtually their whole side suddenly decided to play for other clubs in the town!

Just before the aforementioned game against the 'countrymen', there was much speculation as to which team Mosforth would actually play for, being a member of both. There was subsequently a huge roar from the 'Hallamites' when he ran out in their kit, only for Billy to return to the dressing room and reappear in Wednesday colours, much to the chagrin of Hallam fans and glee of Wednesday supporters! Fans of Hallam accused Mosforth of switching sides for financial gain while Wednesdayites were delighted that the 'little wonder' was in their side – it later transpired that Billy always intended to play for Wednesday, but thought he'd have a bit of fun with the crowd. Unsurprisingly, Billy was on the scoresheet as Wednesday recorded a 5-1 win, on the same day that the club's second team registered ten goals in the Minor Cup. A hard-fought goalless encounter against Notts County at Trent Bridge followed before a meeting of the 'auld enemy' pitched Heeley against Wednesday at Bramall Lane. Despite the emergence of Lockwood Brothers onto the Sheffield football scene, the two combatants remained 'top dogs' in the town and a meeting of the two always generated great interest. However, on this occasion there were no 'bragging rights' for either set of supporters as the Heeleyites snatched a late equaliser to ensure parity.

FRED THOMPSON

Sadly, like so many of his contemporaries, Fred Thompson died at a tragically young age, dying from 'inflammation of the brain' (meningitis) on 2 May 1898, aged just twenty-eight. Born in Sheffield on 17 January 1870, teenager Fred left Wesley College to learn his articles as an architect/surveyor under future Wednesday president Holmes. His rise to prominence in Sheffield football was meteoric as the sturdy curly-headed right full-back was scouted from minor club Hastings, from where he was given a trial game by Wednesday, aged just seventeen. Fred proved the best player on the pitch and signed immediately. His dashing style and brilliant fearless play saw Fred quickly become a first team regular and before long he was handed the captaincy. He quickly became a crowd favourite and forged a full-back partnership with Brayshaw. Throughout his time at Wednesday he remained strictly amateur – playing football purely for pleasure – and was captain when the Alliance was won in 1890, although he was absent due to ill health for a large part of the season. He never really recovered and in September 1890 was found in a state of 'insensibility' on his bedroom floor. He managed the occasional game before moving to Nottingham Forest, for whom he made his solitary league appearance in their first match in the Football League. His health meant he was forced to retire from the game in 1893.

Away from the parochial matters of Sheffield football, the debate regarding professionalism was bubbling in Lancashire, and in November 1884 the Football Association was forced to call a meeting where several northern clubs threatened to form a break away association unless the FA changed their stance of expelling any club from the FA Cup if they were found guilty of playing players. Back in Sheffield, Wednesday lost the return fixture with

Notts County before it was FA Cup time again and a trip into the unknown to face Long Eaton United. For the tie at the Flats ground, Wednesday gave a FA Cup debut to George Wilson and also took the bold move of playing two men at centre forward – Cawley and Winterbottom. In front of a 'very large' crowd the visitors led through a Cawley goal, which was hotly disputed by the Long Eaton players, and this proved enough to earn a place in the next round as Rangers' objection to the result – they alleged the goal should not have been allowed due to a foul – was not sufficient for the FA to order a replay. Two days later, Wednesday progressed in the Sheffield Cup, beating Attercliffe, while the club then arrived late at Nottingham Forest forcing a delayed kick-off, although a mixed Wednesday side recorded a splendid 5-0 success.

The following two Saturdays involved visits to Blackburn to face the previous two winners of the FA Cup, Rovers and Olympic, losing to the former. Unfortunately the second trip saw Wednesday again weakened by Sheffield FA call ups and a seemingly dispirited side lost 12-0, despite the hosts only having ten men and Hunter playing in goal. The defeat sent ripples through Sheffield football, and there was a further sign of a distinct power shift when Lockwood Brothers sent Wednesday tumbling out of the Sheffield Cup at Bramall Lane. Some pride was restored when Blackburn Rovers were held to a draw.

The disastrous day in Blackburn was exorcised on Boxing Day when a much stronger Wednesday side thrashed Olympic 6-0, the visitors having become over confident and sending their reserve side to Sheffield, much to the disappointment and outright indignation of the Wednesdayites. The opening day of 1885 saw progression in the Wharncliffe Cup, admittedly against a Mexborough side that played for most of the game with an injured player, before it was FA Cup action against Nottingham Forest at Bramall Lane. A relatively poor crowd attended the fixture and saw away player Hancock man mark Wednesday star man Mosforth 'like a barnacle to a ship's bottom', resulting in a 2-1 win for the away side.

A win at Astley Bridge and draw at Mexborough preceded a friendly with Bolton Wanderers, which proved highly controversial and probably contributed greatly to Sheffield's continued stance against the 'evils' of professionalism. Wednesday led 2-1 at the interval, but their burly opponents then shocked all present by their 'rough play' and 'win at all costs' attitude, which literally scared the home side into submission in the second half, mainly due to fear of injury. The blatantly biased away umpire also did little to calm fans and after Bolton scored five times without reply, their players were hooted and jeered off the pitch at the end. The majority of the fans' fury was reserved for the away umpire and he had to be shielded by his friends as blows rained down from the furious Wednesday fans as he battled back to the dressing rooms, the whole sorry episode only further strengthening the Sheffield FA's anti-professionalism stance.

J. B. THOMPSON

Very little is known of mid-1880s club secretary J. B. Thompson, as unlike many of his contemporaries he seemingly did not play the game of football; he just helped Wednesday behind the scenes for two years. He was voted into the role of secretary in 1885 – he had previously been treasurer at Fir Vale FC in the early 1880s – and served for a single season before stepping back onto the general committee. He was connected with the club for a further year before cutting ties and later filled the role of secretary to Kimberworth where he lived.

The name of Haydn Morley first appeared in a Wednesday side for the loss to Heeley before it was back to winning ways with a comfortable success over Rotherham at Hunter's Bar. The biggest game of the season for Wednesday – against Preston North End – was next on the fixture list, but it snowed and rained solidly for two days before and the weather conditions continued unabated during the match, which was watched by only 400 fans, the vast majority of whom were huddled together under a newly erected shelter at Bramall Lane. Those that did brave the elements were treated to a masterclass of the 'dribbling game' by Preston, whose attitude, even though they were professional, contrasted markedly from the tactics utilised by Bolton. The display of Preston, who won 4-0, showed the positives of professional football and they further highlighted how Sheffield had fallen behind Lancashire football by registering an 8-1 success in the return game. The Wharncliffe Cup semi-final against Lockwood Brothers at the Old Forge Ground saw Wednesday draft in Derby County men Arthur Latham, Haydn Morley and Frank Sugg, but the game ended all square.

A single goal from Winterbottom was enough to squeeze Wednesday through in the replay, while the final also went to a second game after Wednesday and Heeley could not be separated. A fine display of goalkeeping by Smith helped Wednesday to lose only narrowly to Aston Villa before the club became embarrassed when Nottingham Forest went home with a 7-0 win in a 'complete farce of a match' that saw both Mosforth and Cawley retire injured in the second half and Wednesday yet again arrive late. It was becoming clear that all was not well behind the scenes, and the mood darkened further when old rivals Heeley recorded a convincing 4-0 win in the replayed final of the Wharncliffe Cup. It had been another disappointing season and it ended in April 1885 with a 3-2 win at Ecclesall Road in a benefit game for Malpass. There was no sports day either at Easter as the event had been put back to August Bank Holiday Monday when around

4,000 attended, although a reduced number of entrants was perhaps a sign of diminishing interest.

The summer of 1885 saw a multitude of changes in the administration side of the club as Wednesday kicked off the new season back at the Sheaf House Grounds. The FA Cup draw had paired Wednesday with Long Eaton for the second season running and there was therefore more than the usual interest when the sides met on opening day. Dungworth kicked off the new campaign, kicking uphill towards Bramall Lane. The major talking point from the game, which Wednesday won, came late in the match when an almighty scrimmage ended with the uprights and crossbar being knocked over. Unfortunately, that opening victory would prove a false dawn as what followed was another poor campaign, with another early exit from the FA Cup: A 0-0 game with Lockwood Brothers and defeat to Park Grange, in a match ruined by far too much charging, followed before another understrength side was heavily beaten at Notts County. It was clear that Wednesday could no longer count on Sheffield's best players, shown when Wednesday ambitiously played two games on the same day, at Spital Olympic and Walsall Town, but was heavily beaten in both with neither of the teams fielded including any 'big name' players. Wins against weaker opposition, such as Notts Olympic, preceded a first ever meeting with Owlerton, which Wednesday could only draw. It was then time for the FA Cup and a visit to the new Recreation Ground.

Unfortunately, it was not to be as, on a pitch covered in puddles, Long Eaton totally dominated proceedings and led 1-0 at the break. The visitors then went down to ten men when Mosforth was injured and duly slipped out of the competition with somewhat of whimper, losing 2-0. A defeat at Rotherham did little to lift the gloom, although a 7-1 Sheffield Cup win over minnows Holmes, after a bye in the first round, restored some faith. It would be a long season though for fans as a stalemate with Attercliffe was followed by a shocking 8-2 home loss to Derby County. A first ever meeting with Port Vale – at the Athletic Grounds – caused Wednesday more embarrassment as they arrived with only nine players and had to draft in Betteney (Stoke FC) and Watson (Burslem) before losing 3-0. Thankfully the Sheffield Cup was providing some solace and the club's last ever senior game played at Hunter's Bar ended in a 2-0 win over Hallam on a frosty, slippery pitch – it should be noted that a game against Spital, in February 1886, would have been the final match at the venue, but the game was never played after Wednesday failed to raise a team, much to the annoyance of the visitors. A trio of consecutive draws, versus Nottingham Forest, Heeley and Lockwood Brothers, ended the calendar year although a fourth game against Heeley at Bramall Lane was abandoned after 20 minutes due to a waterlogged pitch. New Year's Day saw a 4-1 victory over Walkley in the Wharncliffe Cup before new opponents (Tottenham) Hotspur were beaten 2-1 in Sheffield. The Sheaf House meeting with Park Grange was abandoned in the second half when visiting player Harrison suffered a broken leg. Wednesday would not win again until mid-March. Despite Derbyshire being badly affected by heavy snow there was not even a 'shovel full' on the County Ground pitch as hosts Derby County won 6-0.

The home game with Walsall Town saw the Wednesday players all wearing mourning badges as a mark of respect for the late William Littlehales, but the losses continued unabated with Town recording a convincing 4-1 win. The snowy winter had already caused the scheduled Sheffield Cup semi-final meeting with Heeley to be postponed twice – the second cancellation was despite a large number of unemployed men clearing the pitch only for a further snowfall to ruin all their efforts. When it did finally go ahead the teams arrived to find the Bramall Lane pitch frozen, but after being allowed to play on another part of the ground it did reach a conclusion, with a late Brayshaw leveller forcing a replay. Despite including the likes of Cawley, Hudson and Dungworth, Wednesday were again thrashed by Halliwell – 9-0 this time – before Preston North End again showed their undoubted qualities by completing back-to-back wins. Thankfully, local cup football had been the one saving grace for Wednesday and they were favourites in the Wharncliffe Cup semi-final against Clinton. However yet more snow caused the match to be postponed and when it was rearranged Clinton had to withdraw, as many of their players could not leave work, with Lockwood Brothers being reinstated. Wednesday played the tie under protest, considering it unfair that they had to play a 'once-beaten' club, and it was probably their indignation that spurred the players to their best result of the season – a resounding 6-0 success.

JIM SMITH

There is no doubt that Jim Smith was the club's first great goalkeeper. Born in Sheffield on 11 April 1863, the 5-foot-9-inch custodian started his career at junior side All Saints, moving to the Nether club when they disbanded. Also a fine cinder track runner, Jim joined Wednesday in 1883 and would become almost ever present for the decade that followed, accruing twenty-two consecutive games in the FA Cup and a further fifty-seven matches in the Alliance. A brave and outstanding shot stopper, Jim appeared in the 1890 FA Cup final and was also ever present as Wednesday won the Alliance League. He was also a real character; during games he would often be seen smoking a clay pipe, which he would throw into the back of his net if his goal became under threat. He was on the club's books when league status was secured but only played reserve football before moving to Rotherham County. Away from football he worked all his life as a steel melter at the Atlas Works of John Brown & Co., eventually becoming melting shop manager and founder member of the Atlas and Norfolk Sports Club. He passed away in 1937 with his place in club history assured.

Long-time adversaries Heeley would play a key role in the final weeks of the season as the sides met in the replayed Sheffield Cup semi-final and also in the final of both the Wharncliffe Cup and the newly introduced Mayor's Relief Charity Cup. The first meeting, the cup semi-final at Ecclesall Road, ended 3-1 to the Heeleyites, although the game was suspended near the end when a disturbance broke out in the corner of the ground and spectators rushed across the pitch: Wednesday's appeal that the field was not suitable and spectators had encroached was not upheld at a subsequent Sheffield FA meeting. Incidentally the appearance of Sheffield FC players, Wilson and Davy, directly led to a letter being received by both parties:

> this committee very much regrets the course adopted by you in playing on March 20th for Wednesday Club in preference to Sheffield Club and feel compelled to point out that any repetition of such conduct will inevitably result in you being left out of the team.

Both remained in Wednesday colours with Davy scoring a week later in a draw with Notts County, although the visitors arrived with only nine men and had to draft the services of Housley. The new tournament, organised after an anonymous gentlemen donated a fine silver cup, was for the best four teams in the town and commenced at the Sheaf House grounds when Wednesday and Heeley progressed. It was therefore time for another Heeley versus Wednesday final, and it was ex-Wednesday man Carl Hiller who came back to haunt his old side as with the score level he grabbed the winner. Wednesday therefore had one last chance of silverware, but it would be Heeley who again stood in their way in the final of the Wharncliffe Cup. The tie was played at Attercliffe's Brightside Lane ground and despite heavy rain throughout the match proved keenly contested, but it was Wednesday who got their noses ahead early on, Mosforth scoring. It was 'rebel' Sheffield player Davy who secured the win, kicking away from the church in the second half and ensuring a great finish to what had been a difficult campaign. The season may have ended in Sheffield, but Wednesday still had one game left to play and this encompassed a first meeting with Everton, resulting in a

3-1 defeat in Liverpool. The summer marked the end for the club's popular sports days with the nineteenth and final one held in August 1886 at Bramall Lane. A healthy crowd again attended and it was rather fitting that the fourteenth race of the day, and last ever event, was won by a Wednesday footballer as Harrison took the honours in the 750-yard steeplechase.

ALBERT CORBETT MUMFORD

Shropshire born in 1865, Albert 'Clinks' Mumford started his football career at village side Wrackward-in-the-Wood before moving to Sheffield in 1881, playing junior football for Bethel United and Berkley Star, scoring double figures for the former in a 27-0 win over Mexborough. A gas stoker, Mumford signed professional forms with Wednesday in 1887 and the attacker served the club for almost a decade, making his FA Cup debut in 1889. He played in every position including between the sticks in an 1891 game versus Sunderland Albion. The popular Mumford appeared in the 1890 FA Cup Final and also played in Wednesday's first game in the Football League. He was capped thirteen times by the Sheffield FA and later in his career was more commonly found in a full-back or half-back role. His loyalty was rewarded with a benefit game in 1896, and he finished his career at then Football League club Loughborough Town after settling there. He lost a long fight against cancer on 30 June 1926.

The 1886/87 season would prove arguably the most important of the pre-league years as off the field events would change the direction of the club immeasurably and result in Wednesday re-emerging as the dominant force in Sheffield. As professionalism started to sweep away the ethos of amateur football, Wednesday remained steadfastly against the idea, but it would be a simple clerical error that would force a change of heart. The mistake involved the club's entry for the 1886/87 FA Cup competition, which was not submitted within the time parameters meaning Wednesday could not compete in the biggest competition in British football. This was another huge blow for Sheffield as despite local football still being well attended the football reputation of the town was declining in both strength and influence, despite Sheffield being the fastest growing provincial town, driven by steel and cutlery, with a 300,000 population. For Wednesday in particular, the season would show that the club was highly competitive in local football but were simply no longer competitive against many of their long-time rivals in 'out of town' games. This was shown in the first half of the season when defeats were suffered at Aston Villa (0-7), Nottingham Forest (1-4), and even Long Eaton (0-4).

The season had opened with a defeat at Attercliffe before Lincolnshire Cup holders Grimsby Town held Wednesday to a draw at their Clee Park ground. A win at Lockwood Brothers and draw with Derby Midland preceded the aforementioned hammering at Villa, despite Wednesday fielding a strong XI. Five days later came the defeat at Forest's Gregory Ground before the Sheffield Cup campaign started with a welcome 3-0 stroll over Eckington Works. Four straight defeats, including a heavy loss at Rotherham, ended with a shocking 6-2 Sheaf House defeat to Staveley – several call-ups to the Sheffield FA again showing how Wednesday could no longer call upon the best talent in the town to 'step into the breach'. Defeats at Clinton and Owlerton, sandwiched progress in the Sheffield Cup, although a poor crowd of only 300 watched the narrow win over Park Grange in the third round, Wednesday having been given a bye to reach that stage. Crowd figures had certainly fallen in general and even a meeting of the two most popular clubs in the town, Wednesday and Heeley, only attracted 2,000 to see the former win. Four goals were shared with Derby County before the year ended with a draw against Heeley, Wharncliffe Cup success over Attercliffe, on a pitch covered with frozen snow, and resounding 4-0 win over London (Tottenham) Hotspur where the pitch was so shrouded in mist that it was commented the 'players looked like phantoms'.

JOHN HUNTER

Without doubt one of the best players of the Victorian age, Jack Hunter was born in Crookes, Sheffield, in 1852 and started his working life on a Norton farm. His football career commenced at the age of eighteen when he joined Heeley and he proved an outstanding half-back. He was quickly made captain by his club and was capped by the Sheffield FA. In the latter part of the decade he played alongside the Clegg brothers for Albion, and when Wednesday entered the FA Cup they secured his services, Jack playing in the club's first tie, although he had played occasionally for Wednesday before, first being noted in a December 1875 game against Broomhall. He later described the conditions for the FA Cup tie at Darwen as the 'most terrible weather he remembered for football'. He was so revered in local football that when he was briefly out of work a benefit match was arranged for him and he was presented with a silver watch bearing the inscription 'Presented for his good captainship and good play, April 1880'. Described as a brilliant defender, Jack was also equally at home at the other end of the field thanks to his superb dribbling skills and while at Heeley he was capped seven times by England. He was also a brilliant all round sportsman, winning the half mile, steeplechase, 500 yards and mile races all in one day at Garrick's sports day in the early 1870s. His talents could not be retained in Sheffield, where he worked as a butcher and silver cutter, and he was lured across the Pennines in 1882, joining Blackburn Olympic. A thinly veiled professional at Blackburn, he is credited with organising a team of amateurs into a potent force and introducing the passing style of play, which would help them win the FA Cup just a year later. He joined rivals Blackburn Rovers around 1887 – playing for them in the opening match at Olive Grove – and later became assistant trainer and groundsman. He is also believed to have briefly coached New Brighton Tower in 1897, helping them achieve league status. Hunter – who Mosforth stated was the best back he had ever seen – remained in Blackburn for the rest of his life, dying of consumption on 9 April 1903, aged fifty-two, while running the Mason Arms in the town.

Unfortunately, the New Year started disastrously as Wednesday arrived at Halliwell with just nine men and played the game with just ten, after procuring a substitute. After just 25 minutes, the home side were 5-0 ahead and an almost unrecognisable side would go on to lose 16-0 – the biggest defeat recorded against a senior Wednesday team in their entire history. Despite the ground having an appearance of a sheet of ice, the result was a huge surprise and the club was urged to 'wake up or your long-established and deserved good name will sink into oblivion'. Two weeks later, there were nine changes made for the Wharncliffe Cup semi-final, with Lockwood Brothers, and a 3-0 win ensured another appearance in the final. The win was not, however, a sign of better times as it was followed by a loss at Mexborough and then a period of four matches in eight days, which started with a Charity Cup final against Staveley. It was a fine day at Bramall Lane for the tie, but the game proved somewhat one sided, with the superb play of Wednesday defender Brayshaw failing to stop his side losing by three clear goals, match referee Charles Clegg no doubt reflecting on the dire straits of his old side. Games on consecutive days probably contributed greatly to a home defeat to Clinton – Wednesday fielding a scratch side – with the 'cup' team saved for the much anticipated visit of Preston North End to Bramall Lane. The Lancashire side did not disappoint, despite being understrength, and delighted the crowd with their speed and splendid passing to register a 5-0 victory. A hat-trick from home forward Heckingbottom then led the 'railway men' of Derby Midland to victory before the club rose to the occasion of the Sheffield Cup semi-finals by surprisingly defeating Lockwood Brothers. It was certainly 'one step forward and two steps back' as a single goal loss at Lincoln City was followed by a second chance of much needed silverware, in the Sheffield Cup final against surprise qualifiers Sheffield Collegiate. Thanks to the work of Bramall Lane groundsman Mr Wright, the pitch was in fine shape for the blue ribbon event of the Sheffield football calendar, and in a topsy-turvy match it was commented that the 'Wednesday defence saved them the match and the forwards almost lost it', eluding to the fact that Wednesday were under pressure for long periods in the game but somehow were still level with 5 minutes remaining, at which point Brayshaw won the cup for Wednesday. It was a much needed shot in the arm and would prove their last trophy as an amateur club as matters were coming to head off the field, with rumours abounding that professionalism would soon come to the fore in the town with or without Wednesday. A few days later, the club held a ball at the Bath Saloon. There was still a couple of games to play, with another trophy on offer for the team that scored most goals in consecutive games against Heeley. This was part of Heeley's sports day and two Cawley goals secured back-to-back wins in a month when he played a much bigger role in the history of the club.

JOHN DAVIS

John 'Plumbstick' Davis was a real character from Wednesday's early years. Born around 1845, Davis was a huge Wednesday fan, and in those far off days it was said that he never missed a home or away game – a remarkable feat for the era. It's believed he started to assist the club with training around 1877 and gained such respect in the ensuing years that he was affectionately called 'father' or 'dad' by the players. It was one of the proudest moments of his life when Wednesday officially recognised his contribution by bestowing upon him the title of assistant honorary trainer – to Wilf Muscroft – meaning he could continue to devote all his free time to Wednesday but also have his expenses reimbursed. Training often involved the players – in normal daily attire – taking a brisk walk around a local reservoir and he was well known for serving his pre-match meal of a 14lb steak, mash and onions! He was 'Wednesday, first, last and all of the time', and the former fishmonger and publican (Lyceum Hotel) continued to assist the club past his sixtieth birthday. Described as a 'big-hearted little man', Davis remained devoted to Wednesday until he passed away on 7 January 1917, aged seventy-two, after having watched Wednesday for one final time on New Year's Day.

Due to Wednesday not playing in the FA Cup, the nucleus of their squad switched allegiance to Lockwood Brothers and helped them to the last sixteen of the FA Cup before losing to West Bromwich Albion. The former Wednesday players were conscious of the potential of a team made up of the best players of Sheffield, and to achieve this aim a new side was formed – Sheffield Rovers. They arranged to play two games at the season's end – one against Heeley on 30 April – which allowed them to apply to enter the FA Cup. An application was duly sent and accepted.

These were troubling times for Wednesday as the best players of the town, although not particularly wanting to turn professional en masse, expressed the desire that if any of their colleagues wanted pay to help meet their expenses then they should have the right to do so. What followed, at the Brunswick Hotel, changed the history of Sheffield Wednesday forever as Rovers met to discuss their options. It was at this meeting that Cawley suggested that Wednesday should be given one final chance to say 'yes or no' on the subject of payments. As the meeting was packed with Wednesday members, they signed a requisition for a special general meeting of the club, which took place at the Garrick Hotel on 22 April 1887. The gathered members duly heard a report from the special committee appointed by Wednesday FC into the subject of professionalism, which read as follows:

> The special committee, having sat twice, sent out a circular to twenty of the most prominent players of the town, who are also members of the club (the circular stated that the committee had a scheme in view to form a very strong and representative club team in the ensuing season, and questions to the terms of which players would join were asked). The committee recommend the registration of professionals to the meeting and that a certain amount be paid to each registered player per match.

The adaption of the report was moved, seconded, supported and carried unanimously with wages set at 5s for home games and 7s 6d for away games. A new era had begun and the *Sheffield Daily Telegraph* commented that 'professionalism is now coming to the fore in Sheffield and it is infinitely better than the thinly veiled secret professionalism which has been rampant amongst us'.

Wednesday Recover Their Status as Sheffield's Best Team

If that momentous decision was not enough for Wednesday supporters to absorb, the club duly announced that they would be moving to a new ground, just off Queens Road. The adoption of professionalism had instantly caused a problem as Wednesday could not sustain a professional wage bill from just members' subscriptions and their relatively small take of any games played at Bramall Lane after the owners had taken their cut. The decision was therefore taken to agree a seven-year lease with the Duke of Norfolk for a swampy piece of land on the southern side of the Midland Railway line. It was said by many that the ground was too far from the centre of town and Wednesday might not even get 200 fans to make the trip, but work quickly started, with the club spending £5,000 to bring the ground up to standard – its previous tenants, Nether FC, had played on a pitch where springs bubbled underneath the surface and the footpath went straight across the pitch.

The path was diverted, the brook covered and a 1,000 capacity covered stand erected on the northwest side of the ground. The venue could be accessed via railway bridges from both Charlotte Road and Myrtle Road. A house that lay a little way to the east of the ground gave Wednesday's new home its name – Olive Grove. The 110 x 70 yards pitch was surrounded by a 6-foot cinder track. Wednesday quickly secured the best local talent and announced season ticket prices of 10s 6d. Initially, Wednesday would change at the Earl of Arundel and Surrey Hotel – their committee room was at the Cambridge Hotel on Cambridge Street – and walked on a sometimes very muddy lane over the railway bridge to the ground, but this was a mere inconvenience as old foes Blackburn Rovers visited, for a £10 guarantee, for the first game. Fears that fans would not travel were quickly allayed as 2,000 attended the Monday afternoon game, with a new chapter in club history beginning at 4.00 p.m. It was Mosforth who scored the first goal at Olive Grove and fans were thoroughly entertained as 8 goals were shared – Wednesday recovering from a 4-1 deficit.

The season had actually started with a defeat at West Bromwich Albion, but overall the club's decision to turn professional and obtain their own ground would be justified although the alternative would have perhaps been too bleak to contemplate.

HAYDN ARTHUR MORLEY

Haydn Morley captained Wednesday in their first FA Cup Final, and was carried from the field shoulder high despite the heavy defeat. The right-back, small in stature but fiercely tenacious, proved a popular leader in his short spell at Wednesday. Born in Derby on 26 November 1860, Haydn played the majority of his football in that region, appearing for both Derby County and Notts County before moving to Sheffield to work as a solicitor around 1889 – he had appeared for Wednesday before that date. He remained strictly amateur throughout his career and was the first signing of Derby County, played in their first fixture and his father, William, actually founded the Rams. He retired from football in the early 1890s and continued to work in the legal profession in Sheffield. He was incredibly still working just after the end of the Second World War. He lost a leg late in his life due to illness, and ran the local Hathersage brass band before passing away, at the grand old age of ninety-two, in May 1953 – the last surviving member of that 1890 Wednesday side.

A heavy defeat to FA Cup holders Aston Villa followed, but the season would be remembered for a double success in local cup football and the re-emergence of Wednesday FC as a force in the 'English' Cup. A hat-trick of victories were then recorded against Lockwood Brothers, Notts Rangers and Sheffield FC, the latter game being the first meeting despite Sheffield being formed a decade before Wednesday. A hotly contested game at Nottingham Forest ended 2-1 to the hosts before Wednesday travelled to Owlerton FC for the first time in a competitive match. The occasion was the first round of the Sheffield Cup and Wednesday were lucky to escape with a replay after the teams shared 6 goals; the hosts denied a winner when the referee deemed the ball had gone out of play. It was then time for the FA Cup and a first ever meeting with Belper Town at their Windmill Lane ground. Wednesday were missing some key players, the likes of Albert Kinman being drafted in for his only senior game, but were ahead inside 30 seconds as Waller found the net. Goals from Kinman and Cawley stretched the lead further and although Town pulled two goals back Wednesday held on to progress. The early goal in Derbyshire would be repeated in the next two games as Cawley put his side one up, inside a minute, as Wednesday beat Owlerton in the Sheffield Cup replay. It was Cawley again who scored early in the home friendly with Mexborough with a one-sided game ending 9-0 to the blue and whites. Big wins over local opposition became a theme for the season as the now professional Wednesday racked up a series of convincing scores over clubs who were still amateur. A week after the Mexborough match, Holmes were beaten 6-0 in the next round of the Sheffield Cup, and before Christmas they'd score 10 against Eckington Works (Sheffield Cup), beat Park Grange 5-1 and also Heeley 7-0 (Wharncliffe Cup). Interspersed between those one-sided games were defeats at Rotherham Town and Burnley, but all eyes were on the next round of the FA Cup, with the club yet again drawn at Long Eaton Rangers.

A special train ferried around 200 Wednesday fans to the game, many embarking at Heeley station, but it looked like they would return home disappointed as the home side led 1-0 at the break, after a hard fought first half. The situation worsened when Carl Hiller was badly injured early in the second half and was a virtual passenger for the remainder of the tie.

WILLIAM INGRAM

Born in Sheffield on 11 December 1866, Billy Ingram was an Attercliffe lad and became a bricklayer, like his father and his three brothers. His football career started with minor club Bethel Reds and he appeared for the likes of Attercliffe and Carbrook Free Church before joining Wednesday late in 1886. The forward netted the first of several hat-tricks in December 1887. He was on the losing side in the 1890 FA Cup Final. He was still at Wednesday when league status was achieved, but all of his eight senior goals in sixteen games came in FA Cup football before he moved to Heeley in 1893. He lived the remainder of his life in Sheffield and was a constant attendee at Owlerton, watching the first team and reserves, although the 'dyed in the wool' Wednesday fan caught a chill watching a game after undergoing an appendicitis operation and never recovered, passing away on 19 March 1949 at his Shiregreen home. On his deathbed Billy asked 'how have Wednesday gone on?' When being told they had beaten Nottingham Forest he said 'that's good' and died.

However, Wednesday did not lie down and late in the day Mosforth levelled, forcing extra-time. It was the turn of Waller to put Wednesday through and send that merry band of Wednesdayites home in celebratory mood. The next round took Wednesday to the unfamiliar surroundings of the Essex County Cricket Club ground, at Leyton, where local club

Crusaders had drawn the northerners in the fourth round – Wednesday having received a bye in the third round. A crowd of less than 1,000 were in attendance, the majority startled when a small band of intrepid Wednesday fans celebrated wildly after Carl Hiller scored what proved to be the only goal. Seven days later, on Christmas Eve, an understrength Derby County side were routed 8-0 and the year ended with another eight-goal haul, this time against Sheffield Collegiate.

The first game of 1888 saw Wednesday back in FA Cup action with a tricky tie at long-time rivals Nottingham Forest in the fifth round. Interest was immense, and the 8,000 crowd included a travelling barmy army estimated at around 2,000. Wednesday man Brayshaw ran onto the pitch proudly wearing his England cap; the men from the 'cutlery capital' were well represented, fielding arguably their strongest side. However, an early goal proved a setback and despite an equaliser from Ingram it was the hosts who led 2-1 early in the second period. An injury to home player Burton then changed the game as he was forced to retire. Wednesday totally dominated the remainder of the tie, scoring three times to progress through, with Ingram grabbing a hat-trick.

On the Monday that followed, Wednesday fielded the exact same side to beat Lockwood Brothers 3-0 while Clinton and Mexborough were beaten 9-0 and 3-0, respectively. Those games were just aperitifs to the main course – a sixth round FA Cup tie against Preston North End – in the first FA Cup tie staged at Olive Grove. In preparation for the match, Wednesday made various improvements to the ground, which included covering the brook that bordered the elevated side of the ground, to make a sloping terrace, a new stand being hastily erected and several drays strategically placed to create further vantage points. However, plans for the cup tie then fell into disarray when medical opinion in Lancashire suggested that, due to an alleged smallpox scare, it would be unwise for a large crowd to gather in Sheffield. When this was dismissed, the Lancashire medical 'experts' suggested that it could be unsafe for the Preston players to play in Sheffield. However, they did not bank on the diligence of Charles Clegg as he visited several local doctors and received assurances that any danger to health would not increase or diminish if the tie was played in Sheffield or elsewhere.

The Challenge Cup committee ruled the tie should go ahead and it did so, albeit delayed by 48 hours from the original date. The Monday afternoon kick-off was expected to affect the gate, but Wednesday fans turned out in their thousands, on a snowy day, with the 9,000 crowd comfortably the biggest attendance seen for a club match in Sheffield. Unfortunately, the tie proved a game too far for Wednesday as the physically stronger North End side secured a 3-1 success, with Ingram netting a consolation goal for the home side. Despite the cup exit, Wednesday was still in both local cup competitions and they duly reached the final of the Sheffield Cup as a

Mosforth header settled the Bramall Lane semi-final against Staveley. A visit
to their old Sheaf House ground followed – now used by Park Grange – and
a 4-0 win ensued, followed by a dress rehearsal of the Sheffield Cup final as
Ecclesfield were beaten at Olive Grove.

A home win over Derby Midland was quickly followed by back-to-back
ties in the Wharncliffe Cup, Wednesday proving a bogey side for Staveley by
knocking them out in the semi-finals again. This set up a Charity Cup final
tie against Rotherham, but arrangements were thrown into confusion, due
to overnight snow, and then descended into chaos after the management
committee conferred and decreed the game would be played, a message
being quickly dispatched to the Rotherham club secretary and public notices
issued. Unfortunately, it did not seem that either the Bramall Lane ground
authorities or Wednesday had any knowledge of the game being given the
'green light', so the decision was quickly reversed. Despite all this, fans and
the Rotherham side arrived at the ground expecting to see a game while a
handful of Wednesday men arrived, blissfully unaware of the postponement!
At this point all the officials conferred again and it was resolved to play the
tie with messages dispatches to all areas of the town to corral the remaining
Wednesday players into the ground. There was subsequently a huge cheer
when last man Betts arrived and the game finally started an hour late. It
did appear foolhardy to play the game as the pitch had not been cleared,
being several inches thick with snow, but the two sides battled on and it was
Wednesday who drew first blood after a Cawley shot hit an upright and
glanced in off a defender. That remained the score until the final minute,

JACK DUNGWORTH

Heeley-born Jack Dungworth, was another example of a player who
gave great service to Wednesday. A right half-back, Jack was said to be
one of the first examples of a 'man marker' as he would often shadow
the opposition's star player, sticking to him 'like a leech'. As a youngster,
Jack had won countless prizes as a runner. He started his football career
at junior side Meersbrook Rangers before joining Wednesday, aged
fifteen, around 1881. He made his senior bow in 1884, and within a few
months Jack, who 'had a kick like a mule', was an automatic choice and
remained so despite remaining amateur when the club turned professional
– he worked as a table knife hafter. An Alliance title followed, plus an
appearance in the 1890 FA Cup final, before he fell down the 'pecking
order' after the arrival of Harry Brandon. He retired around 1892 and
ran the Queens Head Hotel on Bramall Lane until 1895 when he filed for
bankruptcy, citing bad trade and disagreements with his wife. He suffered

personal heartbreak in 1906 when his four-year-old daughter died of fatal burns after playing with matches. Jack passed away, aged seventy, late in 1936.

when Ingram netted to secure a fifth Charity Cup success and the first silverware of the professional era. A week later it was the final of the Sheffield Cup, but this was preceded by the visit of Preston North End for a deserved benefit game for Mosforth, a healthy crowd watching the Lancashire club convincingly beat a Wednesday and District side. Unlike the 1881 meeting with Ecclesfield, the contest in 1888 proved much closer with the opposition having trained in the 'salubrious regions of Matlock' prior to the final. The snow had melted away and it was Ecclesfield who went ahead early on with Hulley (a distant relative of future Wednesday Chairman Geoff Hulley) netting. Wednesday hit back with a magnificent Winterbottom shot, but his side were in arrears at the break after dominating but failing to convert their many chances. It was 2-2 on the hour (Ingram), and then to 'loud cheers from their numerous adherents' Carl Hiller scored the winner as Wednesday again completed the Sheffield Cup double. A game against Notts County had been arranged after Wednesday had beaten their rivals Forest in the FA Cup, and the fixture proved eventful as County raced into a 4-0 lead at Olive Grove, only for Wednesday to storm back and almost grab an unlikely equaliser as the visitors hung on.

A win over Rotherham and a poor 0-0 with Ecclesfield (in a benefit game for a Pitsmoor player who'd broken his collarbone) preceded a friendly at Lincoln City where Cawley was unfairly sent off, only for the referee to realise his mistake. However, as a matter of principle, Tom refused to return and watched from the touchline as his side won 2-1. A touring side – playing under the name of the Welsh Amateurs – were beaten 8-4 before Wednesday shared 4 goals with Halliwell and put 7 past Staveley. Three more friendlies ended the season, with Heeley beaten 4-0 and Wednesday gaining a draw at Derby County where they had home player Haydn Morley in their side. The final game of the season, against Doncaster Rovers at Olive Grove, was postponed due to bad weather but went ahead a week later with Cawley scoring the final goal of the campaign to seal a 3-1 win. It was not the last football that would be seen at Olive Grove though as the club hosted a six a-side competition, offering six silver watches for the winners and the same number of football bags for the runners-up. Eight teams entered – Carbrook Church, White Lane, Staveley, Doncaster Rovers, Wentworth, Rotherham, Derby County and Wednesday – with the hosts receiving a walkover in the first round after a no show from Staveley. The small duration games were played on a beautiful sunny day, with extra points won by gaining corners or putting the ball between posts 4 yards either side of the goals (a direct nod to the old rouge system). Wednesday beat Derby on minor points to reach the final where they comprehensively beat Doncaster by scoring 2 goals and registering 8 minor points to their opponents 0. It signalled the end of what had been a highly successful first season as a professional outfit, with Wednesday reporting they had generated over £827, incurring expenses of £767, despite the FA Cup tie at Crusaders being a financial disaster. The club also decided to issue ground tickets to honorary members, giving the holder and one lady admission to the ground and enclosure for all club matches for a minimal charge. It was also commented that 'the experiment (of turning professional and securing their own ground) therefore must be considered highly satisfactory, both from a financial point of view and in regard to success in playing the game'.

Before the season finished, a pivotal moment in the history of English football took place when at a Manchester hotel, the Football League was formed. Twelve clubs were elected into the competition, with Wednesday, Forest and Halliwell later applying but being refused admission as the league could only see twenty-two vacant days in the football calendar. The new format became an instant hit, with regular, guaranteed and competitive football proving hugely popular. Minor cup ties and friendlies seemed somewhat tame by comparison, which made Wednesday's decision, in July 1888, to withdraw from the Sheffield FA rather baffling. The club noted that in the previous season they had lost players on fourteen occasions to representative games, and while the club bore no antagonism towards the local FA they believed that there was no pecuniary benefit to Wednesday to lose players on so many occasions. There were therefore no Challenge or Wharncliffe Cup matches in 1888/89, with the fixture list limited to a plethora of friendly games and, of course, the FA Cup. In total, Wednesday played forty-nine times during the campaign, which commenced with the visit of FA Cup winners West Bromwich Albion to Olive Grove, where despite a rise in admission prices, to 6d, there was still a healthy crowd, who saw Wednesday lose 3-1 on a pitch that had been widened by around 5 yards in the summer. Incidentally, during the club's Olive Grove years, a fan was appointed, for a small payment, whose job it was to retrieve the match ball when it was kicked over the fence onto the railway line. In later years, mischievous Sheffield United fans suggested the supporter had two speeds: 'go slow' if his side were desperately hanging onto a 1 goal lead, or 'at the double' if they were losing.

With the FA Cup not starting for Wednesday until February due to a new format, fans had to be content with a mixture of club games such as a draw with Nottingham Forest in the first home game, and matches against local sides, which invariably ended with Wednesday winning by big margins. A first ever visit to Doncaster resulted in a 3-1 win, on a ground near to the Deaf and Dumb Institute, before more first time opponents, Witton, were beaten 5-2 at Olive Grove.

JOHN HUDSON

Born in Sheffield on 11 October 1860, Jack Hudson worked as a silver engraver but was also one of the finest footballers in the town during the 1880s, described as 'second to none' in the district. Previous to joining Wednesday he'd appeared for several local sides, including Surrey and Owlerton, but for almost the whole of the 1880s was a rock at the heart of the club's defence. It was said he was 'difficult to pass' and was 'resolute, cool and a sure kicker'. He appeared in Wednesday's first FA Cup tie in 1880. He served on the committee from 1881 to 1886 before being the club's joint secretary, with George Cropper, for a two-year period until 1888. He was also a key figure in the club's adoption of professionalism. In addition to starring for Wednesday, Jack was a fine all-round sportsman and won many prizes on the running track. He also regularly captained the Sheffield FA representative side, and in February 1883 was rewarded with a full cap for England, against Ireland. At the end of his career he was one of the first players signed by Sheffield United, playing in their first game, before injury caused his retirement and a role as trainer back at Wednesday. He was later the landlord of a Wadsley Village public house. After his daughter married ex-Owl Jimmy Spoors, he lived the remainder of this life at the Gateford Hotel in Worksop, passing away on 21 November 1941.

A public practice game between the first team and reserves preceded a stunning 9-4 loss at Birmingham St George's. The surprise FA Cup semi-finalists from the previous season, Derby Junction, proved a big attraction at Olive Grove and 3,000 watched Wednesday grab a notable scalp. A totally one-sided affair then saw Park Grange beaten 13-0. Wednesday then met both Sunderland and the Leeds Association, losing on Wearside and beating the latter in Sheffield. Matches at Nottingham Forest and at home to Halliwell preceded three more overwhelming wins against Notts Rangers, Ecclesfield and Sheffield FC, 8-0, 11-0 and 10-1, respectively. Strangely, those victories became counterproductive for Wednesday as fans started to lose interest in friendly matches, and it became an obvious fact that the club had quickly outgrown local football – a new challenge was thankfully on the horizon.

Meanwhile, the goals continued to flow, with 6 at Lincoln City's John O'Gaunt's ground, although Derby Junction – who played in Britain's first public park, the Arboretum – gained revenge with a 1-0 victory. Victories over Heeley, quick revenge over Birmingham St George's and 4-0 win over Derby St Luke's preceded the much anticipated visit of Preston North End.

The Lilywhites would earn the nickname of the 'invincibles' in this season, completing the league and FA Cup double, and 5,000 fans witnessed one of the best matches ever seen in Sheffield, with deafening roars greeting Ingram's second goal, which proved the winner for Wednesday. In the final seventeen days of 1888, Wednesday played an astonishing six times, commencing with a loss at Derby County in a game reduced to 80 minutes due to a poor pitch before a first meeting with Gainsborough Trinity ended level. Visitors Lincoln City were beaten 5-0 on Christmas Eve, although fans were unhappy at the following home game against Staveley as Wednesday only fielded ten players and lost 3-1. Another first time opponent, Newcastle West End (who merged with East End to form Newcastle United) was beaten on their own ground before 'foreigners' descended on Olive Grove, Wednesday losing 2-1 to Glasgow Clyde. A first meeting with Edinburgh club Hearts caused quite a furore after visiting full-back McQueen lost his temper and was seen to snatch the ball from the

GEORGE WALLER

Born in Pitsmoor, Sheffield, on 3 December 1864, George Waller represented Wednesday for the final three seasons of the 1880s, partnering Billy Betts at the heart of the defence – he first came to Wednesday as a forward, but became better known for his defensive role. He appeared in 16 senior games, scoring twice, and was a major factor in the club winning the Alliance League in 1890. His early football was played with Pyebank and Park Grange while he later signed for Middlesbrough Ironopolis, uniquely playing professionally for both the football and cricket sections. He returned home in 1892 and became reserve team coach at Sheffield United and it was while at Bramall Lane he played county cricket for Yorkshire, taking a wicket with his first ball in 1893. He was a medium pace bowler and appeared in three first class matches, taking four wickets. He continued to play second team cricket for Yorkshire late into the 1890s before concentrating on his role at United. He worked as a physiotherapist and trainer for United until 1931 – also running a sports shop near Bramall Lane – before passing away on 11 December 1937.

referee's hands and raise his arms as if to strike the official. This action was met with howls and hisses from the Wednesday fans with shouts of 'order him off', although home players pleaded his case and he remained on the pitch as his side lost 3-0. A return match with Gainsborough Trinity was almost abandoned due to heavy fog and a freezing pitch, and a week later the club met Newton Heath (Manchester United) for the first time in a game that was put back from Boxing Day. A late goal from Winterbottom proved sufficient for Wednesday before Doncaster Rovers were hit for ten in Wednesday's first tie in the new Gainsborough News Charity Cup.

A week later the blue and whites went into the semi-finals of the new tournament, but finally it was time for the FA Cup and an away tie at Notts Rangers. Despite both Forest and County being at home on the same day, Rangers officials resisted Wednesday's offer of 'liberal terms' to switch the game and were rewarded with a bumper 5,000 gate – 2,000 Wednesdayites travelled on three special trains run by the Midland Railway. The tie started in dramatic fashion after Notts scored inside a minute before a rare goal from defender Thompson levelled the tie. Due to an increasingly bad snowstorm and several pitch encroachments, the referee decided not to play extra time, so it was back to Yorkshire.

The second game, played after a win against Sheffield FC, caused unprecedented scenes in the town as Wednesday decided not to make any special arrangements like they had previously against Preston, and could only watch as Olive Grove was literally swamped with eager supporters – proving again that fans would flock to truly competitive games.

HENRY WOOLHOUSE

Affectionately known as 'Toddles' due to his running style, Harry Woolhouse was a popular winger during the club's early professional years, scoring seven times as Wednesday won the inaugural Alliance League title. Born in Ecclesfield, Sheffield, in 1868, Harry grabbed a personal haul of 5 goals in the club's all-time record win, against Halliwell, and also played league soccer for Wednesday, totalling 21 goals in thirty-five 'senior' games. The former Sheffield FC player also appeared in forty-five Alliance games. He sadly died at the age of only forty-three in 1911.

Although well behaved, supporters knocked one of the gates down and were perched at every vantage point, from access steps to rooftops and from any structure that could provide a view of the pitch. There were around 6,000 inside the ground at kick-off with the visitors proving stubborn opponents, keeping Wednesday out until Cawley scored 5 minutes into the second half. A brace from Dungworth wrapped up the tie and set up another Nottingham game with County travelling for the second round. Around 7,000 attended, but the resultant 3-2 win was marred by a bad injury to Harry Woolhouse, which caused him to be carried from the field and taken to hospital. At the time, early in the second period, it was 2-1 to Wednesday and they extended that lead after 78 minutes and then hung on, with ten men, to win 3-2. After the game, rumours abounded that Woolhouse had died, but thankfully this proved incorrect and he was released the day after. After losing at home to Sunderland and progressing to the final of the Gainsborough Cup, it was back to the FA Cup, but Football League side Wolverhampton Wanderers proved far too strong at their Dudley Road home, with the multitude of travelling away fans disappointed as their favourites exited the competition 3-0, despite the game being level at half-time.

A first home meeting with Burnley saw Wednesday increase their admission price to sixpence, causing a drop in attendance, although the club did record another significant scalp, winning 3-1. The season came to a close with eight games in April, beginning with a visit from Blackburn Rovers for Hudson's benefit game. The match ended all-square before the players and officials retired to the George Hotel where the visitors were thanked for agreeing to come to Sheffield on such 'advantageous terms'. The old rivalry with Heeley then seemed confined to the history books as the Heeleyites were beaten 9-1, reaffirming the gap that had opened between a professional Wednesday and their local rivals. Heavy rain had caused the final of the Gainsborough Cup to be postponed but when it was finally played, almost five weeks later, Wednesday secured the trophy as goals from Waller, Mumford and Winterbottom, plus an own goal, beat Burton Swifts 4-1 at Gainsborough – the losers commenting that it 'was no disgrace to be beaten by a team of Wednesday's calibre'.

A Good Friday defeat at Preston, victory at Newton Heath and home success over Crewe Alexandra preceded the final home game against Staveley, which doubled as a benefit game for Wednesday's professional players. A comfortable win ensued with the season ending with a 5-0 defeat at League club Burnley – a game which in hindsight was probably unwise to have arranged as it did little to further Wednesday's ambitions at the AGM of the Football League, held a few days later at the Douglas Hotel, Manchester. A poll run by the *Athletics News* had seen Wednesday top the list of clubs who should be voted into the league and club representative, Holmes, pointed out that there was no Yorkshire team in the league and that Wednesday owned their own ground.

The bottom four teams were up for re-election for the first but certainly not the last time, the member clubs closed ranks with votes registered

Stoke ten, Burnley nine, Derby eight, Notts County seven, Wednesday four, Birmingham three, Bootle and Sunderland two and Newton Heath one.

Club officials were annoyed by the decision and six days later, at the same venue, Wednesday was the driving force behind the formation of the Northern Counties League, which eventually became known as the Football Alliance League; Holmes was appointed the first president. The other founder members were Birmingham St George's, Bootle, Crewe Alexandra, Darwen, Grimsby Town, Long Eaton Rangers, Newton Heath, Nottingham Forest, Small Heath, Sunderland Albion and Walsall Town Swifts. It would prove another pivotal moment in Wednesday history as they would enjoy their best season of the pre Football League era by winning the inaugural title and reaching the FA Cup Final.

League and Cup Double (Almost)

When fans arrived at Olive Grove in late August 1889, they saw a much improved stadium, with a new stand built at the Heeley end of the ground – the original stand freshly painted in blue and white with the words 'Sheffield Wednesday Football Ground' emblazoned upon the roof. The reason for the visit was a public practice game, which saw the first team forwards face the first team backs, with the remaining places filled by reserves. After another two trial matches, the new season opened with the first Alliance League game, against new opponents Bootle. Wednesday were without Waller, due to cricket commitments, and the suspended Mickey Bennett, while the kick-off was delayed by 55 minutes, after the visitors' train suffered a broken axle. It proved a winning start for Wednesday as a brace from Ingram sealed a 2-1 success. Despite Wednesday charging a 'sixpenny gate', there was still 2,000 to see Wolves beaten, which was followed by an identical result at the Cape Hill Ground, home of Birmingham St George's, in the opening away game in the Alliance.

Torrential rain soaked both players and supporters during a home success over Witton, and it was a bad day at Stoke, with the home side winning 5-0. The club's first Alliance league defeat, at Long Eaton, was greeted with great surprise. Injuries dogged the club in those early weeks to such an extent that, in early October, Brayshaw was between the sticks for a thrilling 2-1 win over old adversaries Blackburn Rovers. A league win against Crewe (6-4) and draw at Small Heath kept the club in the top half of the division, although Bootle – who proved to be Wednesday's main rivals for the championship – gained revenge with a 4-1 victory. The ending of Bennett's suspension proved a catalyst as a day later he made his debut in the 6-0 home romp over Burton Swifts and would eventually net 16 goals in twenty-two games, only finishing behind Ingram (22) in the scoring charts. Centre forward Cawley scored five in the 9-1 league win over Long Eaton (Bennett grabbing four) and this triggered a run of eight consecutive wins, pushing Wednesday into top spot – a position they would not relinquish. The run began with wins over Newton Heath, Grimsby

Town and Small Heath. The scheduled home game against Sunderland Albion was downgraded to a just a friendly due to the poor state of the pitch. The teams met again on Boxing Day, on league duty, and the 1,000 travelling Wednesday fans witnessed a 3-2 win. Wednesday completed a trio of Alliance wins over the Christmas period, with home successes over Nottingham Forest and ten-man Darwen. The winning run continued with the double recorded over Forest before it finally ended as Wednesday lost 4-3 at Darwen.

With Wednesday on top of the league and Olive Grove crowds topping the 5,000 barrier, the advent of the FA Cup was eagerly anticipated, the run commencing with a 6-1 home win over London Swifts. The visitors 'keeper was the man of the match as goals from Bennett (2), Mumford (2), Cawley and Winterbottom secured a place in the next round. Before that tie went ahead, Wednesday welcomed York-based club Clifton, but the game proved ridiculously one-sided – finishing 13-1 to Wednesday – with the visitors arriving with only seven men and having to draft in four locals. Back in the FA Cup, interest was reaching huge levels with an estimated 10,000 record crowd packed into Olive Grove for the second round encounter with Accrington. What followed was another fiercely competitive game that saw Wednesday ahead inside the first 5 minutes, only for the Lancashire side, sporting a natty scarlet and white strip, to equalise just before half time. Wednesday played with only ten men, immediately before and after the interval, but the indomitable Betts soon returned to the fray despite a broken nose! His return visibly rallied Wednesday and a Winterbottom goal proved decisive. The terrific win had a great 'spin off' for stalwart Cawley as 5,793 fans attended his benefit game against Stoke FC, which Wednesday won to maintain a 100 per cent home record.

A shock loss at Crewe followed before Preston North End rolled into town, with the match billed as a clash between clubs that were atop their respective leagues. It was boom time for crowds, with another 6,000 attending to see a thrilling game that ended 5-3 to Wednesday. It was then back to the FA Cup and three games with Notts County despite the first two matches both being decided on the day. The anomaly arose due to the re-emergence of post-match protests, with County successfully appealing the first game, which ended 5-0 to Wednesday at Olive Grove, on the grounds of the pitch being unfit due to extreme weather. The teams reconvened at the same venue, and this time the tie went to County, 3-2, before it was Wednesday's turn to protest on the eligibility of County players Oswalds and Calderhead. Both men were declared 'cup tied' with a third match ordered at the County Ground, Derby. Over 3,500 Wednesdayites swelled the gate to over 10,000 and they were thrilled as goals from Cawley and Winterbottom sealed the club's second appearance in the last four of the cup. However, the issue was still not settled as 24 hours before the semi-final match, opponents Bolton Wanderers did not know who they would be facing at Perry Bar, Birmingham. Thankfully another County protest was dismissed and Wednesday were confirmed winners, thousands travelling from Midland Station while the team had been training in Matlock all week before arriving at their base, the White Horse Public House. A crowd of 15,000 were inside the ground when Mumford kicked off. The game was goalless at half-time, with the players returning to the field after a 5-minute interlude. It was Wanderers who sneaked ahead after 70 minutes, but Wednesday fought back immediately and 2 minutes later the match was all-square after Winterbottom fired home. Minutes later, Mumford put the men from the cutlery town ahead and that's how it stayed, despite a scare when Bolton's late equaliser was disallowed by the match official – Wednesday therefore became the only club to ever reach a FA Cup Final despite losing a match.

Back in the Alliance League, hosts Walsall Town Swifts plastered posters all over town advertising the visit of Wednesday as 'the greatest match of the season'. An understrength away side earned a welcome point after sharing 4 goals. The build up to the FA Cup Final meeting with Blackburn Rovers was not ideal as illness and injury disrupted the side, with key man Winterbottom injured in a particularly bruising 4-3 Alliance win over Grimsby Town. Wednesday spent the days preceding the final at Matlock, but unfortunately Winterbottom received another knock to his ankle, which ruled him out of the final. The big day – 29 March 1890 – saw over 2,000 fans catch special trains to London, the vast majority climbing aboard at just past midnight with the remainder catching the 7.00 a.m. excursion. All the trains departed to packed platforms with shouts of 'Play Up Wednesday' as the club became the first from Yorkshire to play in the final. Those that departed early spent their morning at leisure, seeing all the usual tourist attractions, although it was a sign that some things never change when fans expressed astonishment at the prices charged for refreshments in the capital. Wednesday had travelled down on the Friday, staying at their hotel on the Strand, and on the morning of the game attacker Billy Ingram was asked 'Well Billy, How are you? Are you going to play?' His reply was 'Well, I expect to, but I am not fit'. Despite his lack of fitness he was still in the side that represented the club in their first FA Cup Final:

Smith, Morley, Brayshaw, Dungworth, Betts, Waller, Ingram, Woolhouse, Mumford, Cawley and Bennett.

The crowd inside the Kennington Oval was estimated at 20,000, with the throng described as full of 'Englishmen, foreigners, gentlemen, workers, soldiers, sailors and even a few of the fairer sex'. The teams kicked off, Wednesday wearing a blue jersey with a white rose, plus white knickers, and Rovers in an all-white strip. Back in Sheffield, the match pervaded all aspects of everyday life and hundreds gathered outside shops on Snig Hill and South Street, which posted telegrams every few minutes on the game.

Hundreds also gathered at the club's headquarters, on Charles Street, and everybody was confident that 'good old Wednesday' could bring the cup home. Unfortunately, hopes were quickly dashed as the usually reliable Wednesday 'keeper Smith was at fault twice as Rovers scored two early goals. By half time the game was out of sight as Wednesday trailed 4-0 with fans in the ground and back home left stunned. A goal from Bennett, after 53 minutes, did briefly lift hopes, but it was too little too late as Rovers completed a resounding 6-1 win – a late pitch invasion only briefly delaying the final whistle. It had been a sobering afternoon as Wednesday failed to live up to their reputation, showing only patches of the form that had got them to the top of the Alliance and through to the final. The result was met with great surprise and, although there is no doubt they came up against a superior side, they most lamentably failed to do themselves justice.

WILLIAM BENNETT

William 'Mickey' Bennett came from a notable Mexborough sporting family. His father, William Senior, was a famous cricketer and two of his siblings, Henry and Walter, known as Tip and Cockie respectively, were well-known local footballers. Also related was James 'Iron' Hague, who was the Heavyweight Boxing Champion of England and a hero in the First World War, fighting at the Somme and Passchendale. In November 1892, Mickey played alongside his father and brothers for Mexborough. Mickey's career had started in the early 1880s at Rotherham Town. Mickey generally played at inside-forward or centre-forward, and appeared for Mexborough and Doncaster Rovers before signing professional forms with Wednesday in August 1889.

He did, however, get in hot water as it was alleged he had also signed for Rotherham Town and was subsequently banned for a year. This was later reduced, on appeal, to three months after Bennett claimed he had not actually signed the Rotherham forms. He finally made a delayed debut for Wednesday, and after moving to centre-forward was an automatic choice, helping the club to the Alliance title and scoring in the 1890 FA Cup final. Described as a 'brilliant footballer' and a 'superb header of the ball', Mickey rather surprisingly was only a fringe player in his second season and returned to Mexborough in 1891 after five FA Cup and twenty-one Alliance appearances.

He was working in a glass foundry at the turn of the century, living in Mexborough with his wife and four children, and subsequently joined the Army Service Corps aged fifty-three. He was invalided out in 1917 but never really recovered, being buried with full military honours after passing away on 13 September 1919 aged fifty-seven.

However, unlike today, the cup final was not played at the season's end and Wednesday still had eight fixtures, including four league games, left to clinch the championship. However, there was a 'hangover' from the final as visitors Birmingham St George's recorded a stunning 5-0 win, ending Wednesday's run of twenty consecutive home wins. Wednesday's poor form since the final looked likely to scupper hopes for league honours, but thankfully some of their old spark returned as Walsall Town Swifts were beaten 4-0 to re-establish the club as favourites for the title. The win meant a victory over Sunderland Albion in the final league home fixture would be enough to secure the prize and an expectant 4,000 crowd saw Wednesday produce one of their best 45 minutes of the season as goals from Ingram (2), Hiller and Mumford effectively wrapped up the title before half-time.

The 4-1 lead at the interval proved the final score and fans could celebrate their club's first league championship, the blue and whites eventually finishing four points clear of Bootle after winning the final league game of the campaign at Newton Heath. The backbone of the title success was the ever present Smith, Dungworth and Betts while the club's attackers helped to net 70 goals in just twenty-two games. For the first time in their history, Wednesday finished the season with games in May, losing at Derby County and Blackburn Rovers to end an unforgettable campaign. Incidentally, in early May, the AGM of the Football League met to decide the competing clubs for the new season, with Wednesday listed as one of nine teams who applied for membership. However, it later transpired that they never applied or even sent a representative, and it was probably a missed opportunity as they held a stronger case than any of those applying for membership and common opinion was that Wednesday would have been voted in, if they had attended!

It was no surprise that crowds at Olive Grove soared for the 1890/91 season, but conversely Wednesday's form slumped, finishing bottom after winning only four league games all season. The close season saw Wednesday report that finances were in a healthy state although resources had been drained due to the summer relaying of the Olive Grove turf and buildings works to the pavilion. Wednesday also put the matchday refreshments up for tender, placing an ad in the local press, while the experiment of playing a public practice match was repeated, in August 1890, with four such games taking place – the last one inspired by the early days of the cricket club as the married players faced the singletons. All were held at Olive Grove with Jack Hunter's son, also called Jack, appearing in one. Wednesday made a terrible start to the new campaign, failing to win a game until mid-October, at the twelfth attempt. A couple of draws against Newcastle East End and Middlesbrough Ironopolis, during a mini Northeast tour, was a reasonable start to the campaign and there seemed no reason for worry when Wednesday – wearing their FA Cup Final shirts – shared six goals with Lincoln City, in an entertaining start to the home campaign. However, the defeats then started to mount up as Burnley, Sunderland Albion, Everton, Accrington, Walsall Town Swifts & Notts County all beat Wednesday, who incidentally at Nottingham wore a narrow blue and white striped jersey – the first mention of the club wearing their now familiar kit.

The terrible run of defeats also triggered a new phenomenon, supporters airing their views via the local press! The Wednesday fans were not happy, with almost weekly letters appearing, some blaming the club for loading the start to the season with away trips, some accusing the club of tinkering with the forward line (fans were angry that Ingram had been dropped) and one supporter, who used the nom de plume of 'a disgusted observer', stating that he would not be attending any further matches unless goalie Smith was replaced immediately. The league title and run-up to the cup final had raised expectations and they would be a season-long burden for Wednesday. The first win was highly meritious – a great display from Mumford helping to beat Football League side Burnley at Olive Grove. The newly formed Sheffield United and Wednesday had a very public 'falling out' on the issue of playing home games in the town on the same day – a year earlier a planned first ever 'derby' game fell through after Wednesday officials insisted they should have first pick of ground due to their senior status. The new boys offered to draw lots for choice of ground, but Wednesday refused to budge and the match was never played – a few weeks later, in December 1889, Wednesday accused United of poaching some of their best amateur players as the two rivals butted heads.

The fans' frustrations seemingly boiled over at the home game against Crewe Alexandra, which Wednesday lost 6-4, as before the match started it was found that the home side did not have an umpire and subsequently Mr Wake took charge despite the Wednesday players objecting. It was a scenario that did not end happily, and at the final whistle, after Mr Wake had not appealed against a Crewe goal that was clearly off-side, a mob swarmed around the officials as they left the field. The referee and away umpire were treated respectfully, but Mr Wake had to receive a police escort so he could vacate the dressing rooms and eventually leave the ground. The unruly behaviour of the home fans was condemned by president Holmes, although he also condemned Wake for taking the position initially and then antagonising the crowd at the end of the game – it was a sorry episode for all parties involved. A draw at Wolves and defeat at Birmingham St George's preceded another home loss – to old rivals Nottingham Forest.

A much needed win over Burton Swifts – who had just knocked Sheffield United out of the FA Cup – lifted spirits, but Wednesday just could not string any results together as they duly crashed 7-1 in the Alliance at Darwen. The long-awaited first win in the league finally arrived – at home to Grimsby Town – but a string of defeats followed with the only match of note, historically, being that much delayed first meeting with Sheffield United, played at Olive Grove on Monday 15 December 1890. Two weeks before the game, fans of both sides started to talk about the encounter, and the Olive Grove turnstiles were clicking an hour before kick-off as supporters flooded into the ground. Famous match card seller Billy Whitham was heard to cry 'All the names of each side, a penny', vendors sold sweets, pies and sandwiches and bookies were kept busy as supporters betted heavily. A crowd of around 10,000 watched as United led 1-0 at half-time, only for Woolhouse to level and Winterbottom to grab a late winner to ensure the blue side of Sheffield could celebrate. The win over United certainly boosted Wednesday as they won the next four games, commencing with a 5-1 home success over Middlesbrough. Woolhouse and Mumford both grabbed hat-tricks as Darwen were thrashed at Olive Grove, and Glasgow Battlefield were beaten 3-2, on New Year's Day 1891. A fifth straight win was also against 'Scotch' opposition as Partick Thistle lost 3-2 despite leading 2-0 at the interval. A pitch covered in 5 inches of snow was probably a contributory factor in a heavy reverse at Small Heath before the much anticipated return game with United was played at Bramall Lane, also on a Monday afternoon.

An estimated 14,000 packed into the cricket ground, fans utilising every available vantage point, and Wednesday looked set to complete the 'double' when Ingram and Bob Brandon put them 2 goals ahead, deep into the second half. However, the game was far from over and United stormed back to win 3-2, leaving the Sheffield football public wanting more after two outstanding games. On the following Saturday, the record books tumbled as Wednesday recorded the club's all-time biggest win, 12-0 against Halliwell in the FA Cup. The teams had originally been drawn at Halliwell, but a tempting monetary offer from Wednesday saw the tie switched and goals from Woolhouse (5), Cawley (2), Mumford (2), Bob Brandon, Harry Brandon and Ingram complete a one-sided win on the same day that United lost 9-1 at home to Notts County.

THOMAS, HENRY, ROBERT AND JAMES BRANDON

Four members of the Scottish Brandon family represented Wednesday in the early 1890s. First to join was Robert 'Bob', who made his debut, under the assumed name of Brown, in a friendly at Wolves in 1890. The centre-forward played in Alliance & FA Cup football in what proved his only season at Wednesday but a lack of goals meant he was released and returned north of the Border. Brother, Tom, was also on the club's books for a relatively short time although he did captain Wednesday in their first Football League game, after joining from Blackburn Rovers in 1891. The right-back amassed thirty-eight senior games for Wednesday, although he was the centre of controversy when he was reported to the FA by Wednesday for appearing in a practice game for Blackburn in 1893 – he believed he had signed a two-year deal at Wednesday when in fact it was a very unusual five-year contract. Months of legal machinations followed before he did eventually rejoin Rovers, and he later won a cap for Scotland. Tom was also found guilty in 1896 of being cruel to his wife, having being physically violent on more than one occasion – the judge ordered a separation and there was hilarity in the court when the prosecution described the defendant as being a 'whole back'. The third brother, James, only appeared for Wednesday briefly between 1891 and 1892, accruing only eight appearances in the Alliance, scoring once. He did, however, make appearances in the Football League for both Preston North End and Bootle. It had previously been thought that Henry 'Harry' Brandon was brother to Tom, but recent research has confirmed that he was a cousin of the Brandon siblings. It was Harry who had the greatest impact on club history after strangely also making his debut under an assumed name against Sheffield United in 1890. Born in 1873 in Kilbernie, Harry spend almost eight years at the club, the outstanding half-back amassing 172 appearances plus twenty-nine in the Alliance, scoring sixteen times. He was a huge favourite with Wednesday fans, and after receiving a benefit in 1897 he ended his playing days at Chesterfield, later working at Barnsley Colliery.

Crowd disorder reared its ugly head again, after the home defeat to Newton Heath, when the match referee had to be protected when a section of the crowd made a rush at full-time. Various committeemen, players and policemen protected the official, although all became splattered as the unruly element launched mud at their intended target. The club hoped the problems would not reoccur, a week later, when Derby County arrived in

Sheffield for the next round of the FA Cup. Both sides were struggling at the wrong end of their respective leagues, and Wednesday looked to be heading out when they trailed 2-1 (William Hodder) with only 12 minutes remaining. However, Winterbottom then scored a quick-fire double, to vociferous roars from the crowd, as Wednesday deservedly booked a place in the third round. Friendly defeats to Everton (their first game in Sheffield) and Preston preceded the next round of the competition, which saw another home tie – against West Bromwich Albion. The match would be the club's biggest home fixture of the pre-league era as records for both crowd and receipts were broken, with 16,871 paying for admission, several thousand being in the ground over an hour before the start.

The sixpenny, shilling and half crown stands were quickly filled and fans could be seen perched in trees at the Heeley end of the ground, desperate to see the tie. Despite both sides occupying the bottom rung of their respective leagues, the game was fiercely competitive and would be decided on a turn of events just before the half hour, when Albion took the lead and Wednesday man Mumford departed the field injured. The Wednesday attacker gamely re-emerged after half-time but could not continue and this meant his side played the remainder of the tie with only ten men, eventually losing 2-0.

After falling at the quarter-finals, Wednesday were left to concentrate on improving their league position, which began with a draw at Newton Heath. A deserved benefit for Winterbottom – against Stoke – raised about £2,000, but sadly neither the beneficiary nor his team mates could stop defeats at Grimsby Town and Crewe Alexandra, which left Wednesday in a straight fight with Bootle for the wooden spoon. The teams played out a stalemate at Olive Grove and Wednesday knew that a positive result in Lancashire would probably ensure they avoided the ignominy of finishing last. Sadly the game was a microcosm of the season as Wednesday arrived late, lost Cawley to injury and were beaten 5-0! A win in the next game, against Birmingham St George's, kept hopes alive with Wednesday fans showing remarkable loyalty with over 8,000 in attendance.

A trio of high-profile friendly games followed with FA Cup finalists Notts County beaten before a maiden visit from Celtic, described as 'the clever Irishmen of Glasgow'. A crowd of 7,000 watched Celtic win 3-1 before a defeat at Stoke and win over Sunderland Albion ended the club's Alliance League campaign, with Wednesday in last place. Wednesday then shared six goals with Glasgow Rangers and beat Sheffield United in the Wharncliffe Cup, Wednesday having rejoined the local FA in 1889. The campaign ended in late April when, in an act of generosity, Wednesday hosted a benefit game for neighbours Rotherham Town, who were in serious financial difficulty. A 2-0 win at least finished the season on a high after months of disappointment and frustration, mixed with the occasional highlight.

End of Non-League Days

In May 1891 the Football League met in Manchester, but Wednesday did not apply for admission as they found themselves in 'hot water' due to the transfer of Tom Brandon from Blackburn Rovers. The club was found 'guilty' of poaching Brandon, with the league officially refusing to even recognise Wednesday and also banning their teams from playing matches against them. Wednesday commented at the time that 'the league reserved to themselves the right to carry off the men of any team but they denied others the privilege of returning the compliment'. The FA censured the league a few weeks later and asked them to reconsider their draconian stance – it would be the New Year before Wednesday faced a Football League club. The club's terrible 1890/91 season was attributed to the 'collapse of local talent' and this led to the mass importation of Scottish players, the likes of the Brandons, 'Sparrow' Brown and Gavin Thompson.

Also making his debut was Fred Spiksley, although fans had to wait a few more days to see the new men after the opening practice game was washed out. Five practice games went ahead with the first Blue versus Whites fixture being played at Park Grange and the other four held at Sheaf House. Disappointing defeats at Sunderland and Stockton opened the new season while a win over a Canadian touring side was mainly remembered for an altercation between Wednesday man Woolhouse and visiting defender Dalton, which saw the Canadian get hold of Woolhouse's cheek with his teeth – the duo were eventually parted, but neither was dismissed. Incidentally, just before Wednesday left for their mini Northeast tour, it was reported that a fire broke out at the Ecclesall Road home of club trainer Wilf Muscroft, which was thankfully quickly extinguished, although among the items lost were twelve club jerseys that were the cause of the fire after Mrs Muscroft put them out to dry too close the hearth!

The new campaign also saw the club's reserve side – rebranded Wednesday Wanderers – play their first league fixture, beating Heeley, in the Sheffield and District League. Back at first-team level, a 7-4 win over Lincoln City was followed by a stunning 5-1 loss to Stockton, which again had fans questioning if another season of disappointment was looming. Thankfully, the Alliance campaign opened with an Olive Grove win over Grimsby Town, watched by 9,000, and a two-point haul at Ardwick (Manchester City) in early December pushed Wednesday into second position.

Away from the league, Wednesday faced both Middlesbrough and Middlesbrough Ironopolis, in back–to-back games, while a trip to London encompassed matches against Royal Arsenal and Millwall Athletic. The game against Arsenal was played on a pitch, which was almost totally waterlogged – up to 6 inches deep in places - but the 'Northerners' were far too strong, winning 8-1. It was then back home for a game that boosted the chances of league football for both of the town's professional teams as an astonishing crowd of 22,900 packed into Bramall Lane for the latest instalment of the burgeoning rivalry between old stagers Wednesday and new pretenders, Sheffield United. It proved a nightmare for Wednesday, losing 5-0, with Spiksley later commenting that he remembered nothing of the game, after receiving a heavy knock from United's Bob Cain! However, the defeat did persuade the Wednesday hierarchy to introduce more systematic training methods with all non-working players expected to train for two hours every morning at Olive Grove.

FRED SPIKSLEY

Without doubt the greatest Wednesday player of the nineteenth century, Fred Spiksley only appeared for the club in the final season before their admittance to the league, after agreeing to sign for Wednesday in February 1891 before returning to play out the season with Gainsborough Trinity – he was actually on his way back from Accrington after agreeing to sign for them when he missed the last train home from Sheffield and met Fred Thompson. He was persuaded not to sign for Accrington before he'd spoken to Wednesday, and the rest is history.

Born in Gainsborough on 25 January 1870, the outstanding left-winger possessed remarkable speed, agility and an unerring eye for the goal. Fred would amass 321 senior games for the club, scoring 115 goals, while also playing sixteen times in Alliance football. His achievements cannot be summarised in a couple of paragraphs as he was capped seven times by England, scoring a hat-trick on debut, winning the League Championship and FA Cup with Wednesday (scoring both goals in the 1896 cup win) . He was nicknamed the 'Olive Grove Flyer' by his adoring fans. After his remarkable career at Wednesday came to an end, he travelled the world coaching in Sweden, Germany, Spain, Mexico and Switzerland. He also played the piano in a travelling sketch show, worked as a freelance writer and scout, was employed at a Mexico City bank (Fred was multi-lingual) and worked as a munitions inspector. In addition he was imprisoned in Germany during the First World War, but managed to escape his captors to flee back to England. He was also declared bankrupt during his life, was found guilty of adultery and led FC Nuremburg to the German Cup in the 1920s. However, Fred's passion in life was horseracing, and it was at a Goodwood meeting on 28 July 1948 that he collapsed and died, supposedly after backing the winner. It was perhaps a fitting end to the life of arguably the most fascinating character to have played for Wednesday.

The same month also saw Wednesday score their first penalty kick - Tom Brandon netting in an Alliance defeat at Bootle – after the new rule was introduced into the English game at the beginning of the season – it was initially called the 'kick of death'. Revenge over United was swift, Wednesday winning 4-1 at Olive Grove, while back in the league, Wednesday completed the double over Ardwick - it was a goal-laden holiday period as seven was put past Lincoln City (new 'keeper Bill Allan making his debut after a local cobbler worked all night to make boots big enough for him) and four more past Scots Glasgow Battlefield, prior to an understrength home side sharing four goals with St Mirren.

The New Year also meant the FA Cup and Football League side Bolton Wanderers visiting Olive Grove. However, after arriving at the ground the match official deemed the pitch unplayable – the surface was frozen solid after heavy snow had been cleared – with the teams instead playing a club match after the surface was covered in straw and sand. The teams tried again seven days later and Wednesday produced one of their best 90 minutes of the season as goals from Spiksley (2), Richardson and Brown secured a comprehensive 4-1 win in front of yet another huge crowd of around 17,000. The next round brought Small Heath to Sheffield, with a scrappy first period ending with a Richardson goal between the teams.

However, the second half became overly physical and Wednesday found themselves down to ten men with only 15 minutes remaining when winger Duncan Gemmell was rather surprisingly sent off by the referee. If that was a shock, then Olive Grove was in uproar when, before Gemmell even reached the dressing rooms, the official also ordered Richardson off, leaving Wednesday with only nine men! The home fans were stunned – President Holmes was again forced to play the role of peacemaker – but any serious crowd disorder was averted thanks to Wednesday scoring a second goal, through Thompson, to clinch the win. The fall-out from the fixture resulted in both Wednesday men receiving a one game suspension while Olive Grove was also suspended for two weeks, although the closure was somewhat of an empty punishment as Wednesday did not have a fixture. Within a fortnight Wednesday were back in FA Cup action, the draw taking them to West Bromwich Albion in the third round. A huge contingent of fans followed their team to Birmingham but saw their favourites behind after just five minutes while the eventual cup winners scored again just before half-time. A goal from Richardson kept the tie alive but Albion proved too strong and the cup dream ended. However Wednesday was still capable of securing a second Alliance title, a draw at Newton Heath re-starting their challenge. Unfortunately, any hopes ended at Peel Croft, home of Burton Swifts, when a fair gathering of travelling fans saw their side almost recover from a 4-1 half-time deficit but eventually lose 4-3.

Wednesday would end the campaign in fourth place, five points behind champions Nottingham Forest, after beating Birmingham St George's 4-0 in the final league game – the match only going ahead after Wednesday sent travel expenses, in response to receiving a telegram stating that their opponents were penniless and unable to travel. Incredibly there were still another ten games to play with Spiksley grabbing four in a 9-1 rout of Partick Thistle and Wednesday conceding and scoring 6, at Derby County and at home to St Mirren respectively.

The home game with Bolton Wanderers saw the club pay all the gate receipts, after expenses, to the local medical charities – a direct consequence of the final of Wharncliffe Cup not being held after Wednesday and the organising committee had a very public disagreement. The season ended on the final Saturday of April, although it was a distinctly inglorious finale as Derby and Wednesday played out the only 0-0 game of the season at Olive Grove, which saw both sides reduced to ten men after Jim Brandon and Archie Goodall were sent off for fighting.

All thoughts then turned to a meeting of the Football League held at the Queen's Hotel, Sunderland, on 13 May 1892. Plans to extend the league to sixteen clubs from fourteen, and form a second tier of twelve teams, were to be agreed with several clubs applying for re-election and admittance. In Sheffield, there was great excitement on the streets as fans of both teams waited for news, with a certain hotel, frequented by local journalists, becoming packed and a crowd of people waiting outside. On being asked about the club's prospects, Wednesday treasurer Arthur Nixon said, with a twinkle in his eye, 'Oh, we are certain to get in' and his confidence was well placed as the news came through 'Wednesday in the First Division, United in the Second'. The vote was unanimous in Wednesday's favour; they received the maximum ten votes, with Alliance champions Forest also joining the club in the top division. A new era was about to begin ...

Epilogue

Through the early years of the football club the cricket section remained one of the Sheffield's best, with arguably their finest XI being the 1876 side, which included Ulyett, Armitage, Slinn and Pearson. Wednesday Cricket Club remained strong and competitive throughout the 1880s, but when league cricket started to be introduced, in the late nineteenth century, they decided, or were forced due to losing their wicket at Bramall Lane, against joining the new format. They had been given notice to quit by Sheffield United in 1893 and this effectively was the beginning of the end as over the years that followed, the number of games played by the club started to slowly decrease to the point where only one or two were played, simply to keep the name alive.

Despite being groundless they were always welcomed by Glossop, during their Wake's Week, with their committee, players and spectators always looking forward to their visit. This annual outing helped to take the club into the twentieth century, and a revival looked on the cards when in 1910 the club excavated a 40 x 70 yard plot of land from a hillside, behind Norton Lees church. The new square was christened with a game against the players of Sheffield Wednesday FC in May 1910 (Lance Morley appearing for the cricket club as the footballers won easily), but unfortunately within a few years the club was reduced to just playing a solitary game every summer. A lack of 'new blood' eventually led to long-time member Morley sadly disbanding the old club:

Wound up on 5th September 1924 at the offices of E .Pearce & Co., Sterling Works, Rockingham Street - Lance Morley (member for 45 years) said

'That on 05/09/24, the Wednesday Cricket Club, founded in 1820, be wound up by force of circumstances over which members have no control, that the Cromwell Cup, won by Wednesday cricket and football club in 1867, be presented to the Wednesday Football Club Limited and the Marsden Cup and mounted ball to the Weston Park Museum'

It was not the last act of the Cricket Club as in 2011 retired civil servant Neville Wright reformed the Cricket Club, mainly due to the real possibility of the football club being wound up as financial problems threatened their existence. They won back-to-back promotions in the Mansfield and District Cricket League and have now progressed to level five, playing their home matches at Davy Sports Club on Prince of Wales Road.

Biblography

Brown, T., *The Ultimate F.A. Cup Statistics Book* (1994).

Clarebrough, D. and A. Kirkham, *Sheffield: The Home of Football* (2009).

Clarebrough, D. and A. Kirkham, *Sheffield United Football Club: Who's Who* (2008).

Dickinson J., *100 Years At Hillsborough* (1999).

Dickinson, J., *Sheffield Wednesday Miscellany* (2010).

Dickinson, J. & J. Brodie, *Sheffield Wednesday: The Complete Record* (2011).

Dickinson, J. & J. Brodie, The *Wednesday Boys: A definitive Who's Who of Sheffield Wednesday Football Club 1880–2005* (2005).

Farnsworth, k., *Wednesday!* (1982).

Fishwick, N., From Clegg to Clegg House The Centenary History of the S & H FA (1987).

Murphy, B., *From Sheffield with Love: Celebrating 150 Years of the World's Oldest Football Club* (2007).

Sparling, R.A., *The Romance of the Wednesday* (1926).

General Register Office Birth records 1837 to Present

Heeley History Workshop 1986 to Present

UK Census Records 1841–1911

Sheffield FC Centenary History 1857–1957

Sheffield Trade Directories – Nineteenth Century

Soccer History Magazine

Whites History & Directory of Sheffield - 1833, 1837 and 1857

Whites Gazetteer & General Directory of Sheffield 1852

Sheffield Daily Telegraph (1855–1986)

Sheffield Iris (1794–1848)

The Sheffield Mercury (1807–48)

Sheffield & Rotherham Independent (1819–1938)

www.findmypast.co.uk

www.thewednesdaycc.co.uk

www.sheffield.gov.uk/libraries/archives-and-local-studies/collections/obituaries.html